1

CATALOGUE OF THE
CUNEIFORM TABLETS
IN THE
KOUYUNJIK COLLECTION
OF THE
BRITISH MUSEUM

CATALOGUE OF THE
CUNEIFORM TABLETS
IN THE
KOUYUNJIK
COLLECTION
OF THE
BRITISH MUSEUM

THIRD SUPPLEMENT

by

W. G. LAMBERT

PUBLISHED
FOR THE TRUSTEES OF THE BRITISH MUSEUM
BY BRITISH MUSEUM PRESS
1992

Published by British Museum Press
a division of British Museum Publications Ltd.
46 Bloomsbury Street, London WC1B 3QQ

British Library Cataloguing in Publication Data

Lambert, Wilfred G.
Catalogue of the Cuneiform Tablets in the Kouyunjik Collection of the British Museum. – Third Supplement
I. Title
499.95

ISBN 0-7141-1131-7

Printed and bound in Great Britain by
St Edmundsbury Press Ltd., Bury St Edmunds, Suffolk

PREFACE

In a major work of scholarship, the main bulk of the collection of cuneiform tablets from Kouyunjik was catalogued by Carl Bezold and his descriptions were published in five volumes between 1889 and 1899. A Supplement, prepared by L. W. King, appeared in 1914. This included inscribed material found by King himself during his excavations at Kouyunjik in 1903-1905, some tablets and cylinders allegedly from Kouyunjik that had been purchased, and, in Budge's words, "a series of fragments from the earlier excavations at Kouyunjik which were not previously numbered or incorporated in the Collection". There were fragments not mentioned by Budge and King, and it is these fragments that form the subject of the present catalogue. With the passage of time the value to Assyriology of such fragments has come to be appreciated, and it is gratifying that Professor W. G. Lambert was available and willing to undertake the work of compiling this catalogue.

In collaboration with A. R. Millard, Lambert is already responsible for the Second Supplement to the *Catalogue of the Cuneiform Tablets in the Kouyunjik Collection*. This mainly contained cuneiform texts found by R. Campbell Thompson's expeditions to Nineveh in 1927-1932. At the time of publication (1966), the fragments that form the subject of this volume had been put away and temporarily forgotten. They were brought to the Department's attention again in the 1970s by C. A. Bateman, Senior Conservation Officer, as a result of enquiries by Dr J. E. Reade and C. B. F. Walker. Other Kouyunjik fragments were identified by Dr I. L. Finkel in boxes of Sippar fragments. It is apposite that these fragments should now be made known, and it is anticipated that this publication will be of help and interest to students of the Kouyunjik Collection. It will effectively bring to an end the great task begun by Bezold more than one hundred years ago. Everything has now been catalogued except for a few boxes of very small fragments that are either uninscribed or contain only a few traces of cuneiform signs. It is possible that a few further Kouyunjik items will emerge, principally from among miscellaneous batches of tablet fragments acquired in the 19th century, but it seems unlikely that any large groups of "K" pieces remain to be discovered in the Department.

In his Foreword Lambert has thanked all those who have assisted in the cataloguing, but special tribute must be paid to C. B. F. Walker. He has invested a great deal of time, energy and expertise in the preparation of the volume for press, including data-processing and indexing, and its speedy appearance so soon after Professor Lambert has completed his work is due largely to his efforts. Thanks are due also to Dr W. van Soldt for technical assistance.

J. E. CURTIS
Keeper

DEPARTMENT OF WESTERN ASIATIC ANTIQUITIES
THE BRITISH MUSEUM
November 1991

CONTENTS

FOREWORD

When L. W. King died in 1919 he had been working on the remaining, mostly small pieces of the K collection, apparently with a view to a further volume of the official *Catalogue of the Cuneiform Tablets in the Kouyunjik Collection* and other forms of publication. Some time after his death the small pieces were put away in storage and were ignored for several decades. They came to light again in the 1970s, in trays below the exhibition cases in one of the galleries, and under the publication plans initiated by R. D. Barnett and continued by E. Sollberger it was decided that there should be one final volume of the *Catalogue* devoted to these small pieces. I was invited to undertake the task, and the result is offered herewith.

Those found as a group in the trays under the show cases were all fired by C. A. Bateman, but in more recent years further finds of similar material have added to the total, and these have not all been similarly fired.

The problems of small fragments are of course very considerable. It is impracticable to use computers to identify such pieces, since the ambiguities of cuneiform script and the lack of reconstructed texts to be used as a basis for machine identifications rule out any such method. It is accordingly necessary to rely on the human memory and on aids such as dictionaries and glossaries. Even so the risks are very considerable, and while many such pieces have been finally and certainly identified as proved by the 335 joins recorded here, the ambiguities of the script mean that proposals made from the surviving signs alone, without the identification of known duplicates or close parallels, are hazardous. No doubt some suggestions of genre made here are wrong, perhaps ludicrously so. Question-marks have been used sparingly, not because they would be incorrect, but because one might end with most things so questioned. Users of this volume must make appropriate allowances for the materials. For example, if a certain piece is called "part of a hymn", this might in fact be a hymnic prologue to a Neo-Assyrian royal inscription, so that the category of text is really "royal inscription" rather than "hymn". We can only catalogue what remains, not take into account the missing portions of the tablets. When the pieces are so small it is necessary often to be vague. Such terms as "litany" have been employed rather than trying in every case to be more precise, since that method would surely lead to many errors. Experts in Sumerian cultic texts will be able to select what has been identified as belonging to this general category, and they will be best qualified to select from it things of particular interest to themselves. On occasion it has not been possible to offer more than a division between tablets for learned libraries and tablets from the administrative archives, and on other occasions it has seemed wisest to offer no suggestion at all.

Unless otherwise stated all fragments are in Neo-Assyrian script and in Akkadian language. Of those in other scripts, the Neo-Babylonian are the most common, and when "Bab." is given as the first criterion of description, this always and only refers to the script, meaning Neo-Babylonian. Some of the fragments had on them, from 19th century marking, indications of the collections to which they belonged, e.g. Rm. and 83-1-18. Since they now all have K numbers, these old marks are given in quotation marks after the K number. These marks survive only on the fragments which were not fired. As with all the volumes of the *Kouyunjik Catalogue* save for the *Second Supplement*, there is never an absolute guarantee that every piece came in fact from Kouyunjik. It is always possible that, when material was packed up for shipping in 19th century Iraq, material from casual purchases or other sources was placed in the same boxes as the material from Kouyunjik, no doubt suitably distinguished in some way, but that when the cases were unpacked in London the items got mixed up. And certainly in some instances pieces from Babylonian sites were mixed up in the Museum with the Kouyunjik material before they were numbered. This probably applies to the Late Babylonian pieces catalogued in this volume.

There are still some very small pieces from the K collection not included here, and it is always possible that more such pieces will come to light with further excavation in the nooks and crannies of the British Museum. However, it is hoped that major items will not be involved, and that the cataloguing of the collection can now be considered complete. Occasionally pieces in Neo-Assyrian script turn up in Babylonian collections in the Museum's holdings. C. B. F. Walker, Assistant Keeper in the Department of Western Asiatic Antiquities, has over the years made notes of all such pieces he has come across, and this list from him is included at the end of this volume. In view of the size of the collection, and the difficulties of reading some material in need of cleaning, it would be unwise to affirm that no such further pieces will ever come to light.

Since there is no one scholar with first hand knowledge of all the categories of texts in the K collection, the method of working was first to make transliterations of all pieces on slips of paper. These were then freely available to be taken elsewhere and studied at leisure. Scholars well equipped to identify fragments of particular categories were invited to peruse these slips and mark on them any identifications or proposals as to category. A few scholars have also chosen to look through the actual pieces in the Museum. Also scholars working in the Students' Room have often been shown pieces which seemed to belong to categories of interest to them. In this way many identifications have been made which would not have been made had this volume been the exclusive work of a single scholar. The following list is of those who have made one or more identifications of pieces in this volume. It would be invidious to try to quantify more exactly how much each has contributed, but the name of R. Borger must be especially noted, since in his planned volume on the whole Kouyunjik Collection the present pieces must have their place, and in preparation for that he has done much work and made many identifications and joins. The writer will conclude this Foreword by expressing his thanks to all those on the list beneath, and also to the numerous members of the staff of the Department, past and present, who have contributed to this volume in some way.

B. Alster, J. A. Black, R. Borger, J. A. Brinkman, K. Deller, W. Farber, I. L. Finkel, M. J. Geller, A. R. George, A. K. Grayson, A. Guinan, U. Jeyes, F. Köcher, T. Kwasman, E. Leichty, A. Livingstone, S. M. Maul, W. R. Mayer, S. M. Moren, S. Parpola, J. N. Postgate, J. E. Reade, E. Reiner, M. Roth, W. van Soldt, K. Volk, C. B. F. Walker.

An asterix with a publication reference indicates that the piece is published there

W. G. Lambert
November, 1991

ABBREVIATIONS

AAA	*Annals of Archaeology and Anthropology* (Liverpool).
ABC	A. K. Grayson, *Assyrian and Babylonian Chronicles* (Texts from Cuneiform Sources 1; Locust Valley, 1975).
ABL	R. F. Harper, *Assyrian and Babylonian Letters* I-XIV (London and Chicago 1892-1914).
ABRT	J. A. Craig, *Assyrian and Babylonian Religious Texts* (Assyriologische Bibliothek 13; Leipzig, 1895-97).
ACh	Ch. Virolleaud, *L'Astrologie Chaldéenne* (Paris, 1908-11).
ADD	C. H. W. Johns, *Assyrian Deeds and Documents* (Cambridge, 1898-1923).
AfO	*Archiv für Orientforschung*.
AGH	E. Ebeling, *Die akkadische Gebetsserie "Handerhebung"* (Berlin, 1953).
AJSL	*American Journal of Semitic Languages and Literatures*.
AKA	L. W. King, *The Annals of the Kings of Assyria*, I (London, 1902).
AMT	R. Campbell Thomson, *Assyrian Medical Texts* (Oxford, 1923).
AnSt	*Anatolian Studies*.
AOAT 1	M. Dietrich et al., eds., *Lišān mitḫurti* (Alter Orient und Altes Testament 1, Kevelaer und Neukirchen-Vluyn, 1969).
ArOr	*Archiv Orientální* (Prague).
ASJ	*Acta Sumerologica* (Japan).
ASKT	P. Haupt, *Akkadische und Sumerische Keilschrifttexte* (Assyriologische Bibliothek 1; Leipzig, 1882).
BA	*Beiträge zur Assyriologie* (Leipzig).
Babyloniaca	*Babyloniaca* (Paris).
BAM	F. Köcher, *Die babylonisch-assyrische Medizin* (Berlin, 1963ff.).
BBR	H. Zimmern, *Beiträge zur Kenntnis der babylonischen Religion* (Assyriologische Bibliothek 12; Leipzig, 1896-1901).
BBVO 6	K. Hecker et al., eds., *Keilschriftliche Literaturen* (Berliner Beiträge zum Vorderen Orient 6; Berlin, 1986).
BiOr	*Bibliotheca Orientalis*.
BL	S. Langdon, *Babylonian Liturgies* (Paris, 1913).
BM	British Museum (tablet signature).
Borger, *Asarhaddon*	R. Borger, *Die Inschriften Asarhaddons* (Archiv für Orientforschung, Beiheft 9; Graz, 1956).
Borger, *BAL*^{2}	R. Borger, *Babylonisch-assyrische Lesestücke* (Analecta Orientalia 54; Rome, 1979)

BPO 2	E. Reiner and D. Pingree, *Babylonian Planetary Omens* : part 2: *Enūma Anu Enlil, Tablets 50-51* (Bibliotheca Mesopotamica 2/2; Malibu, 1981).
BWL	W. G. Lambert, *Babylonian Wisdom Literature* (Oxford, 1960).
Campbell Thompson, *PEA*	R Campbell Thompson, *The Prisms of Esarhaddon and Ashurbanipal found at Nineveh, 1927-8* (London, 1931).
CLAM	M. E. Cohen, *The Canonical Lamentations of Ancient Mesopotamia* (Potomac, Md, 1988).
Cohen, *Eršemma*	M. E. Cohen, *Sumerian Hymnology: The Eršemma* (Hebrew Union College Annual Supplements no. 2; Cincinnati, 1981).
CT	*Cuneiform Texts from Babylonian Tablets in the British Museum* (London, 1896ff.).
DA	A. Boissier, *Documents assyriens relatifs aux présages* (Paris, 1894-9).
DT	Daily Telegraph (tablet signature).
Ebeling, *BVW*	E. Ebeling, *Bruchstücke einer mittelassyrischen Vorschriftensammlung für die Akklimatisierung und Trainierung von Wagenpferden* (Berlin, 1951).
Farber, *Ištar und Dumuzi*	W. Farber, *Beschwörungsrituale an Ištar und Dumuzi* (Wiesbaden, 1977).
Farber, *Schlaf, Kindschen, Schlaf*	W. Farber, *Schlaf, Kindschen, Schlaf! Mesopotamische Baby-Beschwörungen und -Rituale* (Winona Lake, 1989).
FAOS	*Freiburger altorientalische Studien* (Wiesbaden - Stuttgart).
Gray, *Šamaš*	C. D. Gray, *The Šamaš Religious Texts* (Chicago, 1901).
Grayson, *ARI* I	A. K. Grayson, *Assyrian Royal Inscriptions* I (Wiesbaden, 1972).
Haupt, *Nimrod-Epos*	P. Haupt, *Das babylonische Nimrodepos* (Assyriologische Bibliothek 3; Leipzig, 1891).
Hunger, *AOAT* 2	H. Hunger, *Babylonische und assyrische Kolophone* (Alter Orient und Altes Testament 2, Kevelaer und Neukirchen-Vluyn, 1968).
IAK	E. Ebeling, B. Meissner, and E. F. Weidner, *Die Inschriften der altassyrischen Könige* (Altorientalische Bibliothek 1; Leipzig, 1926).
Iraq	(Journal of the British School of Archaeology in Iraq, London).
JAOS	*Journal of the American Oriental Society.*
JCS	*Journal of Cuneiform Studies.*
JESHO	*Journal of the Economic and Social History of the Orient.*
Johns, *Doomsday Book*	C. H. W. Johns, *An Assyrian Doomsday Book* (Assyriologische Bibliothek 17; Leipzig, 1901).
JRAS	*Journal of the Royal Asiatic Society.*
KAR	E. Ebeling, *Keilschriftttexte aus Assur religiösen Inhalts* (WVDOG 28, 34; Leipzig, 1919, 1923).

Köcher, *Pflanzen*	F. Köcher, *Keilschrifttexte zur assyrisch-babylonischen Drogen- und Pflanzenkunde* (VIO 28; Berlin, 1955).
Krecher, *Sum. Kultlyrik*	J. Krecher, *Sumerische Kultlyrik* (Wiesbaden, 1966).
Küchler, *Beiträge*	F. Küchler, *Beiträge zur Kenntnis der assyrisch-babylonischen Medizin* (Assyriologische Bibliothek 18; Leipzig, 1904).
Laessøe, *Bīt rimki*	J. Laessøe, *Studies on the Assyrian Ritual and Series bît rimki* (Copenhagen, 1955).
Layard, *ICC*	A. H. Layard, *Inscriptions in the Cuneiform Character from Assyrian Monuments* (London, 1851).
Lehmann, *Šamaššumukîn*	C. F. Lehmann, *Šamaššumukîn, König von Babylonien 668-648 v. Chr.* (Assyriologische Bibliothek 8; Leipzig, 1892).
Lie	A. G. Lie, *The Inscriptions of Sargon II, King of Assyria* Part I: *The Annals* (Paris, 1929).
LKA	E. Ebeling and F. Köcher, *Literarische Keilschrifttexte aus Assur* (Berlin, 1953).
Lyon, *AB* 5	D. G. Lyon, *Keilschrifttexte Sargon's Königs von Assyrien (722-705 v. Chr.)* (Leipzig, 1883).
MMEW	A. Livingstone, *Mystical and Mythological Explanatory Works of Assyrian and Babylonian Scholars* (Oxford, 1986).
Maul	S. M. Maul, *'Herzberuhigungsklagen', Die sumerisch-akkadischen Eršaḫunga-Gebete* (Wiesbaden, 1988).
Menzel	B. Menzel, *Assyrische Tempel* (Studia Pohl, Series Maior 10; Rome 1981).
MIO	*Mitteilungen des Instituts für Orientforschung* (Berlin).
MSL	B. Landsberger, et al., *Materialien zum sumerischen Lexikon* (Rome, 1937ff).
MVAG	*Mitteilungen der Vorderasiatisch-Aegyptischen Gesellschaft.*
NABU	*Nouvelles Assyriologiques Brèves et Utilitaires* (Paris).
NALK	T. Kwasman, *Neo-Assyrian Legal Documents in the Kouyunjik Collection of the British Museum* (Studia Pohl, Series Maior 14; Rome, 1988).
ND	Nimrud (tablet signature, from excavations of the British School of Archaeology in Iraq).
OECT	*Oxford Editions of Cuneiform Texts.*
OIP II	D. D. Luckenbill, *The Annals of Sennacherib* (Oriental Institute Publications II; Chicago, 1924).
Oppenheim, *Glass*	A. L. Oppenheim et al., *Glass and Glassmaking in Ancient Mesopotamia* (Corning, N.Y., 1970).
Oppenheim, *Dreams*	A. L. Oppenheim, *The Interpretation of Dreams in the Ancient Near East* (Transactions of the American Philosophical Society N.S. 46/III, Philadelphia, 1956).
Or.	Orientalia (Rome).
Or.Ant.	*Oriens Antiquus.*

Pallis, *Akîtu*	S. A. Pallis, *The Babylonian akîtu Festival* (Copenhagen, 1926).
Parpola, *AOAT* 5/1	S. Parpola, *Letters from Assyrian Scholars to the Kings Esarhaddon and Assurbanipal*, Part I: *Texts* (Alter Orient und Altes Testament 5/1, Kevelaer und Neukirchen-Vluyn, 1970).
PBS	*Publications of the Babylonian Section, University Museum, University of Pennsylvania.*
Postgate, *NRGD*	J. N. Postgate, *Neo-Assyrian Royal Grants and Decrees* (Studia Pohl: Series Major 1; Rome, 1969).
Postgate, *Taxation*	J. N. Postgate, *Taxation and Conscription in the Assyrian Empire* (Studia Pohl, Series Major 3; Rome, 1974).
PSBA	*Proceedings of the Society of Biblical Archaeology.*
R	H. C. Rawlinson, *The Cuneiform Inscriptions of Western Asia* (London, 1861ff.). Cited as IV *R* or IV R^2 or V R.
RA	*Revue d'Assyriologie et d'Archéologie Orientale.*
Reiner, *Poetry*	*Poetry from Babylonia and Assyria* (Ann Arbor, 1985).
Reiner, *Šurpu*	E. Reiner, *Šurpu* (*Archiv für Orientforschung*, Beiheft 11; Graz 1958).
RIMA 1	A. K. Grayson, *Royal Inscriptions of Mesopotamia, Assyrian Periods*, volume 1: *Assyrian rulers of the Third and Second Millennia BC* (*to 1115 BC*) (Toronto, 1987).
Rm	Rassam (tablet signature).
Rochberg-Halton, *AfO* Beiheft 22	F. Rochberg-Halton, *Aspects of Babylonian Celestial Divination: The Lunar Eclipse Tablets of Enūma Anu Enlil* (*Archiv für Orientforschung*, Beiheft 22; Horn, 1988).
SAA	*State Archives of Assyria* (Helsinki).
SAAB	*State Archives of Assyria, Bulletin.*
SBH	G. Reisner, *Sumerisch-babylonisch Hymnen nach Thontafeln griechischer Zeit* (Berlin, 1896).
Sjöberg, *Mondgott*	A. Sjöberg, *Der Mondgott Nanna-Suen in der sumerischen Überlieferung* (Stockholm, 1960).
Sm	Smith (tablet signature).
STC	L. W. King, *The Seven Tablets of Creation* (London, 1902).
StOr 1	*Commentationes in honorem Knut Tallqvist* (*Studia Orientalia* 1, Helsinki, 1925).
STT	O. R. Gurney, *The Sultantepe Tablets* (London, 1957-64).
TCS 4	E. Leichty, *The Omen Serie Šumma izbu* (Texts from Cuneiform Sources 4; Locust Valley, 1970).
TDP	R. Labat, *Traité akkadien de Diagnostics et Pronostics médicaux* (Paris/Leiden, 1951)
UFBG	W. Mayer, *Untersuchungen zur Formensprache der babylonischen "Gebetsbeschwörungen"* (Studia Pohl, Series Maior 5; Rome, 1976)

Unity and Diversity	H. Goedicke and J. J. M. Roberts, eds., *Unity and Diversity: Essays in the History, Literature and Religion of the Ancient Near East* (Baltimore and London, 1975).
VAB VII	M. Streck, *Assurbanipal und die letzten assyrischen Könige* (Vorderasiatische Bibliothek VII, Leipzig, 1916).
van Dijk	J. J. A. van Dijk, *LUGAL UD ME-LÁM-bi NIR-G̃ÁL* (Leiden, 1983).
VAT	Vorderasiatische Abteilung Tontafel (Berlin tablet signature).
VIO	*Veroffentlichungen des Instituts für Orientforschung* (Berlin).
Volk, *FAOS* 18	K. Volk, *Die Balag̃-Komposition úru àm-ma-ir-ra-bi* (Freiburger Altorientalische Studien 18; Stuttgart, 1989).
Wiggermann, *BPF*	F. A. M. Wiggermann, *Babylonian Prophylactic Figures: the Ritual Texts* (Amsterdam, 1986).
Witzel, *Tammuz Liturgien*	M. Witzel, *Tammuz-Liturgien und Verwandtes* (Analecta Orientalia 10; Rome, 1935).
Woolley, *Carchemish* II	C. L. Woolley, *Carchemish: Report on the Excavations at Jerablus on behalf of the British Museum* II (London, 1921).
ZA	*Zeitschrift für Assyriologie.*
Zikir šumim	G. van Driel, et al., eds., *Zikir šumim : Assyriological Studies presented to F. R. Kraus* (Leiden, 1982).

Literary texts are cited by tablet and/or line numbers according to the following standard editions:

An=Anum	Unpublished edition of W. G. Lambert.
Angim	J. S. Cooper, *The Return of Ninurta to Nippur: an-gim dím-ma* (Analecta Orientalia 52; Rome, 1978).
Anzû	M. E. Vogelzang, *Bin šar dadmē* (Groningen, 1988).
Atra-ḫasīs	W. G. Lambert and A. R. Millard, *Atra-ḫasīs:The Babylonian Story of the Flood* (Oxford, 1969).
Bīt rimki	Unpublished edition of R. Borger et al.
Enūma Anu Enlil	Unpublished edition of E. Reiner.
Enūma eliš	W. G. Lambert and S. B. Parker, *ENUMA ELIŠ: The Babylonian Epic of Creation - The Cuneiform Text* (Oxford, 1966); with restorations.
Erra	L. Cagni, *L'Epopea di Erra* (Studi Semitici 34; Rome, 1969).
Etana	J. V. Kinnier Wilson, *The Legend of Etana, a New Edition* (Warminster, 1985).
Gattung I-IV	E. Ebeling, *ArOr* 21 357-423.
Gilgameš	Unpublished edition of A. R. George.
Ḫulbazizi	Unpublished edition of I. L. Finkel.
Laws of Hammurabi	R. Borger, *BAL*^{2}.

Ludlul	W. G. Lambert, *Babylonian Wisdom Literature* (Oxford, 1960), pp. 21-62.
Lugale	J. J. van Dijk, *LUGAL UD ME-LÁM-bi NIR-GÁL* (Leiden, 1983).
Maqlû	G. Meier, *Die assyrische Beschwörungssammlung Maqlû* (*Archiv für Orientforschung*, Beiheft 1, Berlin, 1937).
Marduk prayer no. 2	Unpublished edition of W. G. Lambert, see *AfO* 19 61ff.
Mīs pî	Unpublished edition of C. B. F. Walker.
^{mul}APIN	H. Hunger and D. Pingree, *MUL.APIN, An Astrological Compendium in Cuneiform* (*Archiv für Orientforschung*, Beiheft 24; Horn, 1989).
Šamaš Hymn	W. G. Lambert, *Babylonian Wisdom Literature* (Oxford, 1960), pp. 121-138.
Šumma ālu	S. M. Moren, The Omen Series "*Šumma ālu*": *A Preliminary Investigation* (PhD. dissertation, University of Pennsylvania, 1978).
Šumma izbu	E. Leichty, *The Omen Series Šumma izbu* (Texts from Cuneiform Sources 4; Locust Valley, 1970).
Šurpu	E. Reiner, *Šurpu* (*Archiv für Orientforschung*, Beiheft 11; Graz 1958).
Theodicy	W. G. Lambert, *Babylonian Wisdom Literature* (Oxford, 1960), pp. 63-91.
Tintir=Bābilu	Unpublished edition of A. R. George.
Udugḫul	Unpublished edition of M. J. Geller.

CATALOGUE

K 16801 +K 8532+8533+8534+16930 etc. (*ABC* p. 139; *JCS* 26 210* and 32 74, 79*), king list. See K 19528.
K 16802 +K 3396+ end of text, Ikrib.
K 16803 +K 3398+ (*AMT* 97 1 1-3), medical.
K 16804 Akkadian proverbs?
K 16805 Colophon to Šumma ālu.
K 16806 +K 15740. Neo-Assyrian colophon.
K 16807 +K 15907. Ashurbanipal colophon.
K 16808 +K 5968+. Medical, with Ashurbanipal colophon.
K 16809 +K 7091+. Ashurbanipal colophon.
K 16810 +K 9785+. Ashurbanipal colophon.
K 16811 +K 7883. Ashurbanipal colophon.
K 16812 +K 7092. Neo-Assyrian colophon.
K 16813 +K 15903. Ashurbanipal colophon.
K 16814 +K 10851. Ashurbanipal colophon.
K 16815 "*ša ina birīt*".
K 16816 Omens.
K 16817 Uncertain.
K 16818 +K 4657+ obv. 2-5, commentary on Enūma eliš.
K 16819 Omens; liver?
K 16820 Omens.
K 16821 Emesal litany, cf. K 8607+, 81-2-4, 207 (*BL* 73).
K 16822 Literary/religious.
K 16823 +K 7439 (*ADD* 303), Neo-Assyrian document.
K 16824 Incantation.
K 16825 Medical.
K 16826 Bilingual incantation, Udugḫul, dupl. 81-2-4, 248 rev.. etc.
K 16827 Literary/religious.
K 16828 Uncertain.
K 16829 Omens.
K 16830 Omens?
K 16831 Sumerian.
K 16832 +K 7968+, dupl. *CT* 17 9 27-35, Asaggig.
K 16833 +K 4473. Royal inscription of Esarhaddon (Borger, *Asarhaddon* pl. 4, p. 111 IV 1-7).
K 16834 Literary/religious?
K 16835 Omens?
K 16836 Bilingual litany.
K 16837 Omens.
K 16838 Uncertain.
K 16839 Omens.
K 16840 (+)K 2406, Udugḫul XVI?
K 16841 Colophon.
K 16842 Bab., "*išātu kāsistī*".
K 16843 Mīs pî?
K 16844 Omens?
K 16845 Bab. Uncertain.
K 16846 Omens.
K 16847 Bilingual prayer.
K 16848 (+)K 3241 (*AAA* 22 pl. 14), Udugḫul.
K 16849 Literary/religious.
K 16850 Emesal.
K 16851 Omens.
K 16852 Medical.
K 16853 +K 2529+ (IV *R* 53) iii 1-3, catalogue of liturgies.
K 16854 +K 256+ (IV *R* 17) obv. 1-5, Bīt rimki.
K 16855 Literary/religious.
K 16856 Omens.

K 16857 Omens.
K 16858 Omens?
K 16859 +K 4562+ (*MSL* IV 3), Emesal Vocabulary I 94-103. See K 17652.
K 16860 Uncertain.
K 16861 Neo-Assyrian legal: conveyance of real estate.
K 16862 +K 4885+, bilingual prayer.
K 16863 Omens.
K 16864 +K 18285, dup. *AGH* pp. 30-32, 19-26, *UFBG* p. 457 27-34, Gula Šuilla.
K 16865 Bab., "nam.búr.b[i".
K 16866 Uncertain.
K 16867 Uncertain.
K 16868 Omens.
K 16869 Ritual for building a house?
K 16870 Omens.
K 16871 Omens.
K 16872 Tamītu?
K 16873 Bab.
K 16874 Omens.
K 16875 Neo-Assyrian composition.
K 16876 Enūma Anu Enlil.
K 16877 Enūma Anu Enlil.
K 16878 Sumerian litany, Maul p. 373, pl. 61*.
K 16879 Colophon.
K 16880 +K 2109+ (*CT* 25 30-31), god list; see K 17081, K 18864.
K 16881 Sumerian?
K 16882 Neo-Assyrian document.
K 16883 Uncertain.
K 16884 Omens.
K 16885 Bilingual Eršaḫunga, Maul p. 254f., pl. 34*.
K 16886 Neo-Assyrian letter.
K 16887 Bilingual.
K 16888 Uncertain.
K 16889 Bab.
K 16890 Omens.
K 16891 Astrological omens?
K 16892 Šumma ālu XLII.
K 16893 Omens.
K 16894 Medical.
K 16895 Ritual.
K 16896 Purity regulations?
K 16897 Lexical?
K 16898 Astrology?
K 16899 Ritual.
K 16900 Literary.
K 16901 Uncertain.
K 16902 +Rm II 330 (*AMT* 55 3), medical.
K 16903 Bilingual?
K 16904 Omens.
K 16905 (+)K 3348, dup. *AGH* 28 9-13, prayer.
K 16906 Omens.
K 16907 Dup. *VAB* VII p. 24 1-4, Ashurbanipal royal inscription.
K 16908 Bilingual?
K 16909 Astrological omens.
K 16910 Bilingual, lament?
K 16911 Ritual.
K 16912 Incantations?
K 16913 Omens.
K 16914 Omens.
K 16915 +K 8934 (Gray, *Šamaš* 20), Bīt rimki?
K 16916 Omens.
K 16917 Literary/religious.
K 16918 Incantation ki.^{d}utu.kam. Bīt rimki?
K 16919 Bilingual?
K 16920 Emesal?
K 16921 Bilingual litany
K 16922 +K 3183+ (*AfO* 19 p. 61), Marduk prayer no. 2.
K 16923 +K 1621a+ (*AKA* p. 52f. iii 38-47), Tiglath-pileser I royal inscription.
K 16924 Sumerian.
K 16925 +K 5181, Emesal bilingual hymn.
K 16926 Bilingual?
K 16927 Literary.

K 16928 Bab.
K 16929 Uncertain.
K 16930 +K 8532+, *JCS* 32 74, 79*. See K 16801.
K 16931 +K 5168+ (*CLAM* p. 401*), Emesal litany.
K 16932 Extispicy?
K 16933 +K 5345, bilingual, dup. *CT* 17 39. See K 17627.
K 16934 +K 223 (*AGH* pp. 24-26 20-23), Šuilla.
K 16935 Bab. Prayer.
K 16936 Omens.
K 16937 Sumerian religious.
K 16938 Cultic.
K 16939 List of personal names?
K 16940 (Dream?) omens.
K 16941 Uncertain.
K 16942 Uncertain.
K 16943 Liver omens, dup. *CT* 20 49 12-16.
K 16944 Religious?
K 16945 Uncertain.
K 16946 Omens.
K 16947 Neo-Assyrian royal inscription?
K 16948 Exorcistic prayer.
K 16949 Neo-Assyrian royal inscription? Names Elam and Susa.
K 16950 Omens? Medical?
K 16951 Omens.
K 16952 Omens.
K 16953 Religious?
K 16954 Prayer and ritual?
K 16955 Sumerian litany.
K 16956 Emesal, cf. K 3345 (*BL* 41).
K 16957 Sumerian prayer.
K 16958 +K 21755. Dup. K 4639 and *ABRT* I 18 obv. 1-11, bilingual incantation.
K 16959 Sumerian litany.
K 16960 "*ṣalam ṭiṭṭi*".
K 16961 Sumerian litany, A'abba ḫuluḫḫa?
K 16962 Dup. *VAB* VII p. 56 87-96, royal inscription of Ashurbanipal.
K 16963 Hymn?
K 16964 Omens.
K 16965 Erra I 69-73, *AfO* 27 77*.
K 16966 Omens?
K 16967 Omens.
K 16968 Neo-Assyrian royal inscription?
K 16969 +K 4488+ (*STC* I 185), Enūma eliš I 44-50.
K 16970 Omens?
K 16971 Uncertain.
K 16972 Literary?
K 16973 Omens?
K 16974 Omens.
K 16975 Omens.
K 16976 Omens? Medical?
K 16977 Uncertain.
K 16978 Ritual?
K 16979 +K 3399+ (*CT* 15 49), Atra-ḫasis I (*AfO* 27 72*).
K 16980 Uncertain.
K 16981 Omens.
K 16982 Bilingual.
K 16983 "^{d}]*be-let-balāṭi*(tin)".
K 16984 Uncertain.
K 16985 Omens.
K 16986 Ashurbanipal royal inscription, dup. *VAB* VII 20-22 111-114.
K 16987 Sumerian? Extispicy?
K 16988 Sumerian religious.
K 16989 Sumerian religious, Maul p. 88.
K 16990 Royal inscription?
K 16991 Omens?
K 16992 "7 *zik-ru*".
K 16993 Sumerian.
K 16994 Hymn?
K 16995 +K 2365+ (*ABRT* I 19-21), Sumerian litany.
K 16996 Astrological omens.
K 16997 Literary/religious.
K 16998 Literary/meteorology.
K 16999 Omens.

K 17000 Colophon.
K 17001 Uncertain.
K 17002 Liver omens.
K 17003 Literary/religious.
K 17004 Religious.
K 17005 Religious.
K 17006 Extispicy?
K 17007 Omens.
K 17008 Bilingual.
K 17009 Dup. *AGH* p. 48 97-102, Šuilla.
K 17010 Royal inscription?
K 17011 Medical?
K 17012 Liver omens.
K 17013 Religious.
K 17014 Liver omens.
K 17015 Omens/medical.
K 17016 Bilingual.
K 17017 Omens.
K 17018 Bilingual.
K 17019 Literary?
K 17020 Omens.
K 17021 Ritual.
K 17022 Bilingual Eršaḫunga, Maul p. 181*.
K 17023 Neo-Assyrian administrative?
K 17024 Bilingual litany, *CLAM* pp. 536ff., Volk, *FAOS* 18 p. 74, pl. V*
K 17025 +K 4931 (*ASKT* pp. 116ff.), bilingual psalm.
K 17026 Ritual.
K 17027 Omens.
K 17028 Sumerian.
K 17029 Omens, dup. *CT* 20 39 14-22.
K 17030 Similar to Šurpu VIII.
K 17031 Liver omens.
K 17032 +K 2259+, Šumma ālu XLII-XLIII (*CT* 40 42-43).
K 17033 Bilingual incantation.
K 17034 Magico-medical?
K 17035 Omens.
K 17036 Bilingual, royal inscription?
K 17037 Uncertain.
K 17038 Omens.
K 17039 Omens/medical?
K 17040 Ritual.
K 17041 Religious?
K 17042 (Medical?) ritual.
K 17043 Ritual?
K 17044 Omens.
K 17045 +K 3890+...18168+21412, Šurpu VIII 59-61.
K 17046 Liver omens.
K 17047 Religious?
K 17048 Literary.
K 17049 Omens?
K 17050 Omens?
K 17051 Balag, colophon (*šal-šu nis-ḫ*[*u*]), cf. J. A. Black, *BiOr* 44 47 B29.
K 17052 Omens?
K 17053 Medical.
K 17054 +K 7138+, Sumerian litany, balag zi-bu-ù zi-bu-ù, *CLAM* pp. 349, 818*.
K 17055 Ritual?
K 17056 Literary/religious?
K 17057 +K 3801 (*BL* 94), balag.
K 17058 Literary/religious?
K 17059 Akkadian Šuilla and ritual.
K 17060 Omens?
K 17061 Ritual?
K 17062 +K 13533, bilingual; exorcistic?
K 17063 Bilingual?
K 17064 Sumerian.
K 17065 Ritual with Sumerian recitation.
K 17066 Uncertain.
K 17067 Literary/religious?
K 17068 Omens.
K 17069 *maṣṣartu* in six lines.
K 17070 Ritual matters.
K 17071 Literary.
K 17072 +K 4631+. Bilingual Eršaḫunga, *JNES* 33 (1974) 290 20-21.
K 17073 Omens?
K 17074 Ritual?
K 17075 Ritual.
K 17076 Omens, cf. *KAR* 452.
K 17077 Bab. Omens?

K 17078 Prayer/incantation.
K 17079 Literary/religious.
K 17080 Omens.
K 17081 +K 2109+, list of Ištar names, see K 16880.
K 17082 Neo-Assyrian administrative?
K 17083 Omens.
K 17084 Gods from the court of Šamaš.
K 17085 Bab. Ritual?
K 17086 Commentary?
K 17087 Enūma Anu Enlil.
K 17088 Medical.
K 17089 Liver omens.
K 17090 Administrative?
K 17091 Bab. Mīs pî?
K 17092 Bab. Omens from stars.
K 17093 +K 2987b. See Wiggermann, *BPF* p. 11.
K 17094 Uncertain.
K 17095 Enūma eliš VII 54-60.
K 17096 +K 191+. See Küchler, *Beiträge* pl. iv.
K 17097 Ritual.
K 17098 Medical?
K 17099 Uncertain.
K 17100 Uncertain.
K 17101 Uncertain.
K 17102 "*šu-pu-ul*, kala.ga".
K 17103 Omens.
K 17104 Uncertain.
K 17105 Uncertain.
K 17106 Omens.
K 17107 Ritual for quietening a baby, Farber, *Schlaf, Kindschen, Schlaf*, p. 130f., pl. 15*.
K 17108 Uncertain.
K 17109 +K 2869+. Saggig, *CT* 17 25 14-19.
K 17110 Uncertain.
K 17111 Incantation.
K 17112 Omens.
K 17113 +K 3349+, Marduk's Address (*AfO* 19 pl. 25). See K 18488.
K 17114 Tamītu or Ikrib?
K 17115 Ritual?
K 17116 Omens.
K 17117 Literary?
K 17118 Omens.
K 17119 Literary?
K 17120 Ritual?
K 17121 Uncertain.
K 17122 Uncertain.
K 17123 +K 3517+, bilingual Eršaḫunga, Maul p. 216, pl. 33*.
K 17124 +K 3445+, Enūma eliš V 146-156.
K 17125 Literary.
K 17126 Religious?
K 17127 Religious ("*tēdištu*").
K 17128 Uncertain.
K 17129 Uncertain.
K 17130 Medical?
K 17131 Liver omens.
K 17132 Uncertain.
K 17133 About a ghost.
K 17134 Ritual.
K 17135 Literary Neo-Assyrian. Marduk's Ordeal?
K 17136 Uncertain, with Ashurbanipal colophon.
K 17137 Medical?
K 17138 +K 18489. Administrative document or letter.
K 17139 Bilingual.
K 17140 Ritual?
K 17141 Bilingual.
K 17142 Uncertain.
K 17143 Exorcistic, with Sumerian incantation.
K 17144 Bilingual hymn?
K 17145 Bilingual.
K 17146 Mentions "horse".
K 17147 Literary/religious.
K 17148 Ritual.
K 17149 Bilingual or Akkadian incantation.
K 17150 Literary/religious.

K 17151 (+) 1905-4-9, 393, bilingual incantation, dup. *CT* 17 36 88ff. Cf. K 20384+.
K 17152 Omens.
K 17153 Omens.
K 17154 Medical prescriptions, (+)K 9066 (*AMT* 38 3).
K 17155 Uncertain.
K 17156 Omens?
K 17157 Magic?
K 17158 +K 5026+, bilingual incantation, to *CT* 17 4-8.
K 17159 Explicit Malku?
K 17160 Omens.
K 17161 Uncertain.
K 17162 Emesal litany, dup. K 5351.
K 17163 Omens?
K 17164 Sumerian.
K 17165 Liver omens.
K 17166 +K 2544+, Maqlû V 150-155.
K 17167 Omens.
K 17168 +K 2725+, bilingual exorcism, *AOAT* I 12 208-212. See K 18151.
K 17169 Literary/legal?
K 17170 Omens.
K 17171 Uncertain.
K 17172 Omens?
K 17173 Medical.
K 17174 +K 3517+, bilingual Eršaḫunga, Maul p. 216, pl. 34*.
K 17175 Uncertain.
K 17176 Literary/royal inscription?
K 17177 Medical.
K 17178 Medical (drugs).
K 17179 Uncertain.
K 17180 Medical?
K 17181 Bilingual?
K 17182 Omens?
K 17183 Uncertain.
K 17184 Omens (end of tablet).
K 17185 Medical.
K 17186 Bab. Religious.
K 17187 Middle Assyrian. Uncertain.
K 17188 Omens.
K 17189 Omens.
K 17190 Omens.
K 17191 Omens.
K 17192 Omens?
K 17193 Uncertain.
K 17194 Exorcism?
K 17195 Uncertain.
K 17196 Literary/religious.
K 17197 Ritual.
K 17198 Ritual.
K 17199 Uncertain.
K 17200 +K 9618, bilingual Eršaḫunga, Maul p. 66, pl. 5*.
K 17201 Magic
K 17202 +K 6032+, bilingual incantation, Bīt rimki, House IV.
K 17203 Bab. Omens.
K 17204 Medical.
K 17205 Bab. Ritual.
K 17206 Uncertain.
K 17207 Uncertain.
K 17208 Literary?
K 17209 Omens.
K 17210 Uncertain.
K 17211 Bilingual.
K 17212 Dup. *VAB* VII pp. 50-52 16-23, Ashurbanipal royal inscription.
K 17213 Iqqur īpuš?
K 17214 Extispicy.
K 17215 Explanatory list?
K 17216 Uncertain.
K 17217 Omens?
K 17218 Omens.
K 17219 Omens?
K 17220 Uncertain.
K 17221 Uncertain.
K 17222 + K 17753. Emesal litany.
K 17223 Incantation?
K 17224 Omens.
K 17225 Incantation?
K 17226 Uncertain.
K 17227 Related to Enūma Anu Enlil LVI.
K 17228 Omens.

K 17229 Omens?
K 17230 Omens?
K 17231 Medical.
K 17232 Literary/religious.
K 17233 Dup. *TDP* p. 44-46, medical, about the eyes, cf. K 17333.
K 17234 Omens.
K 17235 Literary.
K 17236 Omens?
K 17237 Uncertain.
K 17238 Prayer?
K 17239 Uncertain.
K 17240 Cultic.
K 17241 Uncertain.
K 17242 Astrological omens?
K 17243 Omens?
K 17244 Cultic.
K 17245 Omens.
K 17246 +K 7654, *BWL* p. 251, bilingual proverbs.
K 17247 +K 4555+18160+18467, *MSL* XVI pp. 158-9, Nabnītu XVII 165-171.
K 17248 Omens/magic?
K 17249 +K 2854, Enūma eliš VII 1-5.
K 17250 (+)K 11802(+)20472+20505 +20521. Bilingual hymn to Meslamta'e'a, dup. K 4995+19762 (*ASKT* no. 20) (+)20289.
K 17251 +K 18928. Emesal litany, dup. *SBH* p. 93 obv. 6ff. (*CLAM* pp. 255 5-12; Krecher, *Sum. Kultlyrik* pp. 119-120). See also K 19782.
K 17252 Exorcistic.
K 17253 Omens.
K 17254 Bab. Astrology? Cf. K 9098, *BPO* II 50.
K 17255 Ritual?
K 17256 Omens
K 17257 Bilingual.
K 17258 Sumerian.
K 17259 Emesal hymn/prayer.
K 17260 Bilingual.
K 17261 Bilingual or omens.
K 17262 Literary/religious.
K 17263 Uncertain.
K 17264 Omens
K 17265 +K 2725+, bilingual exorcism, dup. *ASKT* no. 11; R. Borger, *AOAT* 1 p. 12 212-218.
K 17266 Ritual.
K 17267 Omens?
K 17268 Omens.
K 17269 Uncertain.
K 17270 Omens.
K 17271 Bab. Astrological omens.
K 17272 Omens?
K 17273 Medical.
K 17274 Uncertain.
K 17275 Literary/religious.
K 17276 Omens?
K 17277 Religious/omens?
K 17278 Omens?
K 17279 Uncertain.
K 17280 Bilingual Saggig, dup. *CT* 17 26 68-72.
K 17281 Medical.
K 17282 +K 2442, bilingual litany, *SBH* p. 90.
K 17283 +K 2823+, Šuilla, *AGH* pp. 6-8, 20-23.
K 17284 Bilingual litany, dup. *SBH* p. 31 4-14 (*CLAM* p. 321).
K 17285 Uncertain.
K 17286 Astrological omens.
K 17287 "*ḫabaṣirānu*".
K 17288 Omens, dup. BM 53085, cf. K 17375.
K 17289 Bab. Omens?
K 17290 Emesal hymn/prayer.
K 17291 Lines beginning "*aran*".
K 17292 Uncertain.
K 17293 Medical.
K 17294 Bilingual.
K 17295 Medical.
K 17296 Bab. Uncertain.

K 17297 Omens.
K 17298 Omens.
K 17299 Omens?
K 17300 Prayer followed by ritual.
K 17301 Bilingual, Cassite or II Isin?
K 17302 Omens in large, coarse script.
K 17303 Sumerian literary.
K 17304 Omens?
K 17305 "*ina* gig-*šú*".
K 17306 Neo-Assyrian royal inscription?
K 17307 Neo-Assyrian administrative, grant/census.
K 17308 Omens.
K 17309 Instructions (technology?).
K 17310 Medical, cf. *AMT* 14 5 12-13.
K 17311 Omens?
K 17312 Literary/religious?
K 17313 (+)K 15984, Angim 165-168.
K 17314 Omens.
K 17315 Sumerian, literary/religious.
K 17316 Uncertain.
K 17317 Medical.
K 17318 Šurpu III 29-36, cf. Sm 239+.
K 17319 Omens.
K 17320 Sumerian, penitential psalm.
K 17321 Medical.
K 17322 Sumerian, literary.
K 17323 Omens.
K 17324 +K 17325. Omens.
K 17325 See K 17324.
K 17326 Literary/religious.
K 17327 Omens.
K 17328 +K 11619, astrological omens.
K 17329 Bilingual.
K 17330 Liver omens.
K 17331 (+)K 15282. Astrological omens.
K 17332 Omens.
K 17333 Part of *TDP* Tablet 5 (pp. 44-46), cf. K 17233.
K 17334 Omens?
K 17335 Laws of Hammurabi III 54-65.
K 17336 Omens.
K 17337 Omens.
K 17338 Omens.
K 17339 Uncertain.
K 17340 Omens.
K 17341 Omens.
K 17342 Uncertain.
K 17343 Gilgameš XI 163-169.
K 17344 Toothache incantation, dup. *CT* 17 50, etc.
K 17345 Omens?
K 17346 Literary.
K 17347 Bilingual litany, dup. *PBS* I/2 125.
K 17348 Omens.
K 17349 Liver omens.
K 17350 Omens.
K 17351 Portents?
K 17352 Medical?
K 17353 Uncertain.
K 17354 Astrological omens.
K 17355 Omens.
K 17356 Uncertain.
K 17357 Omens.
K 17358 Medical.
K 17359 Uncertain.
K 17360 Medical.
K 17361 Uncertain.
K 17362 Uncertain.
K 17363 Medical or omens.
K 17364 Omens.
K 17365 Magic?
K 17366 Astrological omens.
K 17367 Uncertain.
K 17368 Medical.
K 17369 Uncertain.
K 17370 Uncertain.
K 17371 Uncertain.
K 17372 Bilingual lament, cf. *ZA* 40 84f.
K 17373 Bilingual, hymn?
K 17374 Uncertain.
K 17375 Bab. Omens, similar to K 17288, which see.
K 17376 Uncertain.
K 17377 Ritual and prayer.
K 17378 Omens.

K 17379 Uncertain.
K 17380 Hymn.
K 17381 Uncertain.
K 17382 Omens.
K 17383 Religious.
K 17384 Omens or list?
K 17385 Bilingual litany, dup. *SBH* p. 14, *CLAM* pp. 81 122-125, 821*.
K 17386 Dup. K 2296 (*UFBG* p. 519), Šuilla prayer.
K 17387 Omens?
K 17388 Uncertain.
K 17389 Uncertain.
K 17390 Uncertain.
K 17391 Dup. *CT* 16 11 V 38-45, (+)K 2355+, Udugḫul IV. Cf. K 21762.
K 17392 Medical?
K 17393 Omens.
K 17394 "*iqribanni*".
K 17395 Uncertain.
K 17396 Omens?
K 17397 Names Ur and Nippur.
K 17398 Bab. "*rît*]*i u mašqi*[*ti*".
K 17399 Omens?
K 17400 +K 5040+ (*CLAM* pp. 468ff.), Sumerian litany.
K 17401 Uncertain.
K 17402 +K 3311 (*CLAM* pp. 668ff.), Bilingual litany (not K 17400 as B. Alster, *BBVO* VI 20 n. 4).
K 17403 Astrological omens.
K 17404 Uncertain.
K 17405 Astrological omens.
K 17406 Literary/religious.
K 17407 Catch-line of prayer to goddess?
K 17408 Literary/religious.
K 17409 Sumerian litany.
K 17410 Liver omens?
K 17411 Uncertain.
K 17412 Bab.
K 17413 Liver omens.
K 17414 Omens?
K 17415 Bilingual exorcism.
K 17416 Uncertain.
K 17417 Astrological omens (Šamaš).
K 17418 Uncertain.
K 17419 Omens?
K 17420 Prayer.
K 17421 Literary/religious.
K 17422 Bilingual.
K 17423 Uncertain.
K 17424 Bab. +K 5337+18651+19380. Dup. CLAM pp. 441-442 16-25 and K 19277. Bilingual litany.
K 17425 Sumerian?
K 17426 Uncertain.
K 17427 "u]d.13.kam".
K 17428 Uncertain.
K 17429 Literary/religious.
K 17430 Ninurta hymn, Sumerian.
K 17431 +K 12822+ (*CT* 39 41 8-13), Šumma ālu XCV.
K 17432 Omens.
K 17433 Uncertain.
K 17434 Uncertain.
K 17435 Omens.
K 17436 Uncertain.
K 17437 Ritual.
K 17438 Omens.
K 17439 Omens (Šumma ālu?).
K 17440 Omens.
K 17441 +K 4045b+ (*OECT* VI pl. XVIII), bilingual prayer, Maul p. 184 7-12.
K 17442 Omens?
K 17443 Uncertain.
K 17444 Omens?
K 17445 Dedication of a manufactured object.
K 17446 Liver omens.
K 17447 Ritual?
K 17448 Uncertain.
K 17449 Omens.
K 17450 Omens.
K 17451 Exorcistic.
K 17452 Uncertain.

K 17453 Uncertain.
K 17454 "*šaplānu*".
K 17455 Dup. *SBH* p. 115 (*CLAM* p. 818*, pp. 637ff.), bilingual litany. Cf. K 17927, K 19827.
K 17456 Late Middle Assyrian royal inscription?
K 17457 Uncertain.
K 17458 Sumerian literary.
K 17459 Omens.
K 17460 Medical?
K 17461 Omens.
K 17462 Lexical, temple names.
K 17463 Uncertain.
K 17464 Omens?
K 17465 Omens.
K 17466 Omens?
K 17467 Bilingual.
K 17468 Uncertain.
K 17469 "*lilsu*[*m*".
K 17470 Prayer?
K 17471 Royal inscription of Ashurbanipal, dup. *VAB* VII p. 56 80-85.
K 17472 Uncertain.
K 17473 Omens.
K 17474 Literary/religious.
K 17475 Neo-Assyrian royal inscription?
K 17476 Omens?
K 17477 Cf. Maqlû I 42-43.
K 17478 Dup. Marduk prayer, *Iraq* 31 83 38-47, probably same tablet as K 3151b; cf. K 20155.
K 17479 +K 4615 (*OECT* VI pl. XVIII) + K 20098. Bilingual.
K 17480 Literary/religious.
K 17481 Astrological omens.
K 17482 Literary/religious.
K 17483 Omens?
K 17484 Bilingual?
K 17485 "*šá* egir *a-ḫa-m*[*eš*".
K 17486 Uncertain.
K 17487 Literary/religious.
K 17488 Omens.
K 17489 Religious(?) and colophon.
K 17490 Uncertain, with colophon.
K 17491 Uncertain.
K 17492 Extispicy?
K 17493 Uncertain.
K 17494 Omens.
K 17495 Uncertain.
K 17496 Omens.
K 17497 Medical.
K 17498 Literary?
K 17499 Medical.
K 17500 Omens.
K 17501 Uncertain.
K 17502 Bab. Medical?
K 17503 Hymn.
K 17504 Lexical(?); cf. *MSL* I p. 34 18-19.
K 17505 Omens.
K 17506 Uncertain
K 17507 Ritual.
K 17508 +K 9258 (*Or*. 36 pl. XVI), Gula Hymn of Bulluṭsa-rabi 180-183.
K 17509 Uncertain.
K 17510 Uncertain.
K 17511 +K 12774 (*CT* 40 14), Šumma ālu IX.
K 17512 Omens?
K 17513 Omens?
K 17514 Uncertain.
K 17515 Medical.
K 17516 Historical? Royal inscription?
K 17517 Uncertain.
K 17518 Omens?
K 17519 Dup. *AGH* p. 130 1-7, Šuilla to Ištar.
K 17520 Sumerian?
K 17521 Literary/religious.
K 17522 Uncertain.
K 17523 Dup. Lú = ša I 196-201 (*MSL* XII 102).
K 17524 Colophon.
K 17525 +K 3455+, Neo-Assyrian ritual (Menzel II, T 93ff.); cf. K

17648, 18029, 18117, 18309, 18440.
K 17526 Uncertain.
K 17527 "*egirātēšu*".
K 17528 Bab. Literary/religious.
K 17529 Stars.
K 17530 Bilingual.
K 17531 Literary/religious.
K 17532 Bilingual religious.
K 17533 Bab.
K 17534 Medical.
K 17535 Liver omens.
K 17536 Uncertain.
K 17537 Colophon ("son of Šamaš-bārī").
K 17538 Gattung I, dup. *ArOr* 21 373-4 i 49 - ii 4.
K 17539 Days of month listed.
K 17540 Literary/religious.
K 17541 Bilingual incantation, dup. BM 64270.
K 17542 Omens.
K 17543 Omens.
K 17544 Bilingual proverbs?
K 17545 Religious.
K 17546 Incantation?
K 17547 Uncertain.
K 17548 Medical.
K 17549 Sumerian, omens?
K 17550 Sumerian, incantation?
K 17551 Extispicy?
K 17552 Ritual.
K 17553 Omens.
K 17554 Omens?
K 17555 Uncertain.
K 17556 Omens.
K 17557 Omens.
K 17558 Uncertain.
K 17559 Omens.
K 17560 Uncertain.
K 17561 Bilingual.
K 17562 Liver omens.
K 17563 Omens.
K 17564 Omens?
K 17565 Omens.
K 17566 "*gulgullatum*".
K 17567 Omens.
K 17568 Omens.
K 17569 Uncertain.
K 17570 Bilingual?
K 17571 Dup. K 5173 (*CLAM* p. 816*), Emesal litany (op. cit. p. 234 233-238).
K 17572 Omens.
K 17573 Ritual.
K 17574 Ritual?
K 17575 Omens.
K 17576 Ritual.
K 17577 Omens.
K 17578 +K 3452+, Theodicy 53-57.
K 17579 Bīt rimki, House III A.
K 17580 Uncertain.
K 17581 Uncertain.
K 17582 Royal inscription?
K 17583 Medical?
K 17584 Uncertain.
K 17585 Bab. Catalogue of texts.
K 17586 Sumerian religious, "Ningiku".
K 17587 Omens.
K 17588 Dup. *VAB* VII 16 32-37, annals of Ashurbanipal.
K 17589 Sumerian liturgical.
K 17590 Medical ritual.
K 17591 Enūma eliš VII 87-91.
K 17592 Hymn?
K 17593 Prism fragment.
K 17594 Omens?
K 17595 Prayer to goddess.
K 17596 Literary/religious.
K 17597 Omens?
K 17598 Literary/religious.
K 17599 Omens.
K 17600 Bilingual hymn.
K 17601 Literary/religious.
K 17602 Omens.
K 17603 Omens.
K 17604 Omens?
K 17605 Uncertain.

K 17606 Omens.
K 17607 Neo-Assyrian oracle question, *SAA* IV 146*.
K 17608 Medical.
K 17609 Omens.
K 17610 +K 3481+, dup. *CT* 17 31-32, Alam-níg-sag-íl-la.
K 17611 Sumerian litany, Ukkinta ešbar tilla, Cohen, *Eršemma* no. 27, cf. *CLAM* pp. 479ff.; J. A. Black, *BiOr* 44 47.
K 17612 Sumerian.
K 17613 Tamītu or related.
K 17614 Royal dedication?
K 17615 Literary/religious.
K 17616 Uncertain.
K 17617 Sumerian hymn?
K 17618 Literary?
K 17619 Omens.
K 17620 Omens or ritual?
K 17621 +K 9216, medical.
K 17622 Neo-Assyrian letter?
K 17623 Literary/religious.
K 17624 Uncertain.
K 17625 Omens.
K 17626 Omens.
K 17627 +K 4900+... (*CT* 17 38-40) +K 17680+18121+20383+21190, bilingual incantations, Mīs pî?. See K 16933, 19796 and 20269.
K 17628 Uncertain.
K 17629 Administrative, list of valuable items.
K 17630 Neo-Assyrian administrative?
K 17631 Bab. Extispicy.
K 17632 Astronomy/astrology.
K 17633 "*mēšari*".
K 17634 Magic ("[Asal]luḫi")?
K 17635 Dup. K 8268+ (*AMT* 65 3) 10-13, Šumma ālu CIII.
K 17636 Coarse Bab. Omens.
K 17637 Omens?
K 17638 +K 224+, *CT* 16 5 192-200, Udugḫul 3.
K 17639 Ritual?
K 17640 (+)K 5007+, dup. *CLAM* pp. 385-6 32-35, bilingual litany, A'abba ḫuluḫḫa. See K 18643.
K 17641 Uncertain.
K 17642 Uncertain.
K 17643 Omens.
K 17644 Bilingual Eršaḫunga, Maul p. 374, pl. 61*.
K 17645 Omens.
K 17646 +K 4618, dup. Witzel, *Tammuz Liturgien* p. 138 46-14, bilingual litany.
K 17647 +K 9917, dup. *AfO* 19 64 77-82, Marduk prayer no. 2.
K 17648 +K 3455+. See K 17525.
K 17649 Emesal.
K 17650 Coarse Bab.
K 17651 Neo-Assyrian oracle question, *SAA* IV 113*.
K 17652 +K 4562+, dup. *MSL* IV 5, Emesal Vocabulary I 18-30. See K 16859.
K 17653 Uncertain.
K 17654 Bab. Omens?
K 17655 Bab. Astrology.
K 17656 Ritual and recitation.
K 17657 Sumerian litany, A'abba ḫuluḫḫa, dup. *CLAM* pp. 386-387 49-60, cf. K 18643.
K 17658 Uncertain.
K 17659 Omens.
K 17660 Bab. Enūma Anu Enlil.
K 17661 Bilingual, psalm?
K 17662 Omens.
K 17663 Omens.
K 17664 Lexical.
K 17665 Dup. *AKA* 64 IV 52-55, royal inscription of Tiglath-pileser I.
K 17666 Literary/religious.
K 17667 Religious (bilingual?).
K 17668 Prayer.
K 17669 "*ḫabburru*".
K 17670 End of text with 60xX+28 lines.

K 17671 Literary/religious.
K 17672 Omens.
K 17673 Omens.
K 17674 Uncertain.
K 17675 Sumerian? Religious.
K 17676 Omens.
K 17677 Ritual.
K 17678 Eršaḫunga or other incantation?
K 17679 Literary/religious.
K 17680 +K 4900+, *CT* 17 40, bilingual incantations. See K 17627.
K 17681 Sumerian or bilingual.
K 17682 Sumerian or bilingual.
K 17683 Ritual?
K 17684 Omens or myth?
K 17685 Bilingual?
K 17686 Omens.
K 17687 Uncertain.
K 17688 Uncertain.
K 17689 Omens.
K 17690 Uncertain.
K 17691 Omens?
K 17692 "*barīri*".
K 17693 Bab.
K 17694 Uncertain.
K 17695 Uncertain.
K 17696 Sumerian, lament?
K 17697 Emesal litany.
K 17698 Omens.
K 17699 Medical?
K 17700 Uncertain.
K 17701 Omens.
K 17702 Omens.
K 17703 Medical.
K 17704 Prayers.
K 17705 Ritual.
K 17706 Restoration of Emeslam (by Ashurbanipal? Cf. *VAB* VII p. 186).
K 17707 Sumerian incantations.
K 17708 Religious.
K 17709 Prayer?
K 17710 Bab.
K 17711 Prayer?
K 17712 Sumerian incantation.
K 17713 Omens.
K 17714 Neo-Assyrian administrative.
K 17715 Uncertain.
K 17716 Omens.
K 17717 Uncertain.
K 17718 Sumerian?
K 17719 Omens?
K 17720 Omens.
K 17721 Omens.
K 17722 Uncertain.
K 17723 Royal inscription?
K 17724 Medical.
K 17725 Sumerian, Enlil and Ninlil 68-75, *JAOS* 103 49*.
K 17726 +K 5016, *OECT* VI pl. I, Emesal psalm.
K 17727 Omens.
K 17728 Omens.
K 17729 Uncertain.
K 17730 Uncertain.
K 17731 "*tuquntu*".
K 17732 Omens.
K 17733 Omens?
K 17734 Omens.
K 17735 Uncertain.
K 17736 Neo-Assyrian letter?
K 17737 Bilingual incantation, cf. *CT* 16 39.
K 17738 Uncertain.
K 17739 Uncertain.
K 17740 Religious.
K 17741 Sumerian.
K 17742 Uncertain.
K 17743 +K 2016a+, Urra=ḫubullu IV 161-166 (*MSL* V 165).
K 17744 Uncertain.
K 17745 Bab. Uncertain.
K 17746 Sumerian or omens?
K 17747 Omens.
K 17748 Uncertain.
K 17749 Uncertain.
K 17750 (+)Sm 325? Bilingual litany.
K 17751 Omens?

K 17752 Atra-ḫasīs I, 289-295, 301-302 (*AfO* 27 75*).
K 17753 +K 17222, which see.
K 17754 Bilingual?
K 17755 Uncertain.
K 17756 Uncertain.
K 17757 Omens.
K 17758 Coarse script. Administrative. Offerings?
K 17759 Omens?
K 17760 Uncertain.
K 17761 Coarse script, administrative. Grant/census.
K 17762 Hymn/prayer.
K 17763 Neo-Assyrian royal inscription?
K 17764 Omens.
K 17765 Uncertain.
K 17766 +K 1728, restores *AfO* 23 41 25-30; fire incantation.
K 17767 Sumerian.
K 17768 Bilingual?
K 17769 Uncertain.
K 17770 Uncertain.
K 17771 Bilingual?
K 17772 Omens.
K 17773 Ritual.
K 17774 Uncertain.
K 17775 Bilingual?
K 17776 Uncertain.
K 17777 Omens?
K 17778 Medical.
K 17779 "*išid-su*".
K 17780 Bab. Ritual.
K 17781 Related to the Lamaštu series?
K 17782 Bilingual incantation.
K 17783 Literary/religious.
K 17784 Omens or Sumerian?
K 17785 Colophon to Iqqur-īpuš.
K 17786 Bilingual.
K 17787 Uncertain.
K 17788 Large, coarse script.
K 17789 Uncertain.
K 17790 Udugḫul IX, dup. *CT* 16 39.
K 17791 Uncertain.
K 17792 Uncertain.
K 17793 Omens?
K 17794 +K 215+ (*CT* 25 20), An=Anum III 189-199.
K 17795 Hymn.
K 17796 Neo-Assyrian administrative, grant/census?
K 17797 Dup. *AfO* 19 62, Marduk prayer no. 2, 17-24.
K 17798 Mentions "Assyria".
K 17799 Neo-Assyrian legal.
K 17800 Ritual?
K 17801 Large, coarse script. Neo-Assyrian document.
K 17802 Large Bab.
K 17803 Large, well-spaced script.
K 17804 Hymn.
K 17805 Large Bab.
K 17806 Omens.
K 17807 +K 2373+ (Laessøe, Bīt rimki pl. 2), Bīt rimki, House V. Catch-line to *OECT* VI p. 52.
K 17808 Fire incantations, dup. *AfO* 23 42 III 1-4.
K 17809 Ashurbanipal royal inscription? "The Elamite".
K 17810 Uncertain.
K 17811 Omens?
K 17812 "*k*]*urummat šarri*".
K 17813 Uncertain.
K 17814 Dup. IV *R* 29 no. 1 rev. 12-17 (Udugḫul II).
K 17815 Dup. *CT* 17 6 17ff. (Asaggig).
K 17816 Bab. Ikrib.
K 17817 Bilingual?
K 17818 Cultic?
K 17819 Neo-Assyrian dialect.
K 17820 Literature or royal inscription?
K 17821 Medical.
K 17822 Šumma izbu?
K 17823 Uncertain.
K 17824 Religious, "Kusu".
K 17825 Uncertain.
K 17826 Commentary?

K 17827 Uncertain.
K 17828 Hymn or myth?
K 17829 Religious?
K 17830 Large, well-spaced script. Literary/religious.
K 17831 Mentions "horses".
K 17832 Uncertain.
K 17833 Bilingual.
K 17834 Large, well-spaced script. Mentions the town Ashur.
K 17835 Bilingual.
K 17836 Uncertain.
K 17837 Uncertain.
K 17838 Literary/religious.
K 17839 Uncertain.
K 17840 Liver omens.
K 17841 Dup. *CT* 16 37 34-37, Udugḫul.
K 17842 Enūma eliš I 34-42.
K 17843 Uncertain.
K 17844 Uncertain (very large, coarse script).
K 17845 Uncertain.
K 17846 Ikrib?
K 17847 Omens.
K 17848 Bilingual?
K 17849 +K 4562 (*MSL* IV 6-7 35-39), Emesal Vocabulary I.
K 17850 Uncertain.
K 17851 Uncertain.
K 17852 Uncertain.
K 17853 Atra-ḫasīs I 203-208 (*AfO* 27 74*).
K 17854 Neo-Assyrian royal inscription?
K 17855 Very large, coarse script.
K 17856 Uncertain.
K 17857 Literary/religious.
K 17858 Uncertain.
K 17859 Bab. Prayer?
K 17860 Omens?
K 17861 Theodicy 254-257, (+)K 3452+.
K 17862 Ritual.
K 17863 Letter?
K 17864 Omens.
K 17865 Omens.
K 17866 Omens.
K 17867 Omens.
K 17868 Omens.
K 17869 Incantations.
K 17870 Literary?
K 17871 Šumma ālu LVIII, not excerpts like *CT* 41 18 17ff.
K 17872 Uncertain.
K 17873 Omens.
K 17874 Uncertain.
K 17875 Prayer.
K 17876 Uncertain.
K 17877 Omens.
K 17878 Omens.
K 17879 Uncertain.
K 17880 Magic?
K 17881 Omens.
K 17882 Magic or medical.
K 17883 Šuilla prayer?
K 17884 Omens.
K 17885 Bilingual litany, *CLAM* p. 577 380-383.
K 17886 Omens.
K 17887 Uncertain.
K 17888 Omens.
K 17889 Bab.
K 17890 Literary.
K 17891 Bilingual litany, dup. Cohen, *Eršemma* p. 125 1ff. Cf. K 18655.
K 17892 Uncertain.
K 17893 Omens?
K 17894 Unusual script. Names Šamaš-šuma-ukîn.
K 17895 Omens.
K 17896 Uncertain.
K 17897 Theodicy?
K 17898 Sumerian.
K 17899 Omens.
K 17900 Sumerian.
K 17901 Royal inscription of Ashurbanipal, dup. *VAB* VII pp. 146-8 19-22.
K 17902 Medical.

K 17903 Omens.
K 17904 Omens.
K 17905 "ušburruda".
K 17906 +K 2959+, Šurpu III 75-81.
K 17907 Sumerian incantation.
K 17908 +K 2547+, "Dämonenkopf-Inschrift" (R. Borger, *AfO* 17 358f.).
K 17909 Extispicy.
K 17910 Omens?
K 17911 Uncertain.
K 17912 Exorcism.
K 17913 Liver omens.
K 17914 Bilingual.
K 17915 Omens.
K 17916 Omens.
K 17917 Omens.
K 17918 Sumerian.
K 17919 Omens.
K 17920 Omens.
K 17921 Neo-Assyrian legal, conveyance.
K 17922 Incantation prayer to Marduk.
K 17923 Exorcistic.
K 17924 Omens?
K 17925 Omens.
K 17926 Omens.
K 17927 Dup. *SBH* p. 115 13-19 (*CLAM* p. 639 24-27), bilingual litany. Cf. K 17455.
K 17928 "*itammi*".
K 17929 Omens.
K 17930 Omens.
K 17931 Ritual (medical)?
K 17932 Liver omens.
K 17933 Omens?
K 17934 Neo-Assyrian administrative?
K 17935 Literary?
K 17936 Literary?
K 17937 Uncertain.
K 17938 Uncertain.
K 17939 Watches of the night.
K 17940 Ritual involving Kulla.
K 17941 Hymn.
K 17942 Medical.
K 17943 Uncertain.
K 17944 Omens.
K 17945 Wisdom?
K 17946 Sumerian.
K 17947 Curse formulae?
K 17948 Ritual and prayer?
K 17949 Ritual?
K 17950 Lugale 382-386, ed. van Dijk, pl. lxxiv*.
K 17951 Medical.
K 17952 End of 36-line omen(?) text, about cats (sa.a^{meš})
K 17953 Prophecy?
K 17954 Medical.
K 17955 +K 1284 (*CT* 17 29 17-22), Alam.níg.sag.íl.la.
K 17956 Medical.
K 17957 Sumerian.
K 17958 Hymn.
K 17959 +K 15785, Ashurbanipal colophon.
K 17960 Omens?
K 17961 Omens.
K 17962 Bab.
K 17963 Similar to K 17939.
K 17964 Literary/religious.
K 17965 Literary/religious.
K 17966 Sumerian?
K 17967 Omens.
K 17968 Uncertain.
K 17969 Omens.
K 17970 Uncertain.
K 17971 Uncertain.
K 17972 Neo-Assyrian royal inscription?
K 17973 Neo-Assyrian royal inscription.
K 17974 Uncertain.
K 17975 Omens, lexical or administrative?
K 17976 Ikrib.
K 17977 Literary/religious.
K 17978 Colophon of Nabû-zuqup-kīna.
K 17979 Medical.
K 17980 Uncertain.
K 17981 Omens?
K 17982 "Ištar".

K 17983 "*bu-u*]*p-pa-ni-š*[*u*".
K 17984 Maqlû-type incantation.
K 17985 Uncertain.
K 17986 Literary/religious.
K 17987 Uncertain.
K 17988 Uncertain.
K 17989 Bab. Bilingual?
K 17990 +K 4245, *MMEW* p. 176 and pl. II*, expository text.
K 17991 Uncertain.
K 17992 Literary/religious or bilingual?
K 17993 Uncertain.
K 17994 "Ninkilim".
K 17995 +K 5150 (*BA* 10 p. 108), dup. *SBH* p. 37 9-15. Bilingual litany.
K 17996 Literary/religious.
K 17997 +K 439 (*ADD* 474), Neo-Assyrian legal.
K 17998 Omens?
K 17999 Neo-Assyrian royal inscription?
K 18000 Dup. *ASKT* p. 129 28-35 (*CLAM* pp. 577f. 385-389; Volk, *FAOS* 18 p. 8, pl. IX*). Bilingual litany.
K 18001 Religious.
K 18002 Omens.
K 18003 Uncertain.
K 18004 Omens.
K 18005 Middle Assyrian script.
K 18006 Prayer to Zarpānītum.
K 18007 Letter(?) or expository text.
K 18008 (+)K 10014, 11334+14055, 79-7-8, 38, Malku=šarru II 270-276.
K 18009 Uncertain.
K 18010 Literary/religious.
K 18011 Omens?
K 18012 Coarse script.
K 18013 "ká.silim.ma".
K 18014 Omens?
K 18015 Omens.
K 18016 Omens.
K 18017 Uncertain.
K 18018 Medical.
K 18019 Medical, dup. *TDP* Tablet XIII i 5´-9´.
K 18020 +K 6765+ (*CT* 41 2), Šumma ālu.
K 18021 Dup. *CT* 11 49 9-13, Diri IV.
K 18022 Literary/religious.
K 18023 Uncertain.
K 18024 Omens.
K 18025 Omens.
K 18026 Large, coarse script.
K 18027 Large, coarse script. Letter?
K 18028 Uncertain.
K 18029 +K 3455+. See K 17525.
K 18030 Literary/religious.
K 18031 Medical?
K 18032 Ritual?
K 18033 Uncertain.
K 18034 Omens.
K 18035 Liver omens.
K 18036 Bab. Sumerian?
K 18037 Uncertain.
K 18038 Uncertain.
K 18039 Uncertain.
K 18040 Uncertain.
K 18041 Fable?
K 18042 (+)Sm 308, Šurpu III 137-141.
K 18043 Uncertain.
K 18044 Uncertain.
K 18045 Šurpu IX 71-78.
K 18046 Bab. Uncertain.
K 18047 "Ṣalbatānu".
K 18048 Uncertain.
K 18049 Uncertain.
K 18050 Uncertain.
K 18051 Bab. "Esagil", "Marduk".
K 18052 Uncertain.
K 18053 Names "Ashur".
K 18054 Neo-Assyrian dialect.
K 18055 Extispicy.
K 18056 Uncertain.
K 18057 Dup. Borger, *Asarhaddon* p. 82 19-21. Royal inscription.
K 18058 Uncertain.

K 18059 Bab. Bilingual prayer.
K 18060 +K 2419+ i 17-20 (*AMT* 36 2), medical.
K 18061 Bab.
K 18062 Coarse script.
K 18063 Uncertain.
K 18064 Colophon.
K 18065 Uncertain.
K 18066 Omens.
K 18067 Omens?
K 18068 Uncertain.
K 18069 Omens.
K 18070 Prophecies or omens.
K 18071 Medical.
K 18072 Bilingual, prayer?
K 18073 Omens.
K 18074 Omens.
K 18075 Uncertain.
K 18076 Literary/religious?
K 18077 Extispicy.
K 18078 Uncertain.
K 18079 Listing of gods in sequence.
K 18080 +K 2470+, Udugḫul VI 28-31, cf. *CT* 16 30.
K 18081 Uncertain.
K 18082 Private ritual?
K 18083 +K 13736. Royal inscription of Ashurbanipal, dup. *VAB* VII p. 8 62-67.
K 18084 Uncertain.
K 18085 Omens.
K 18086 Bab. Omens.
K 18087 Uncertain.
K 18088 Omens.
K 18089 End of 81-line text.
K 18090 Omens.
K 18091 Bilingual.
K 18092 Hymn/prayer?
K 18093 Bilingual prayer.
K 18094 "*išdi kussî*".
K 18095 Religious/literary?
K 18096 Royal inscription of Esarhaddon, dup. Borger, *Asarhaddon* p. 88 10-18.
K 18097 Cultic/literary.
K 18098 Religious/literary.
K 18099 Colophon, "[Šamaš]-bārī".
K 18100 Library text.
K 18101 +K 13337 (*STC* I 166), list of Marduk names.
K 18102 Uncertain.
K 18103 Adad hymn?
K 18104 Uncertain.
K 18105 Uncertain.
K 18106 Uncertain.
K 18107 Uncertain.
K 18108 Dup. *JNES* 15 132-134 26-38, Lipšur litanies.
K 18109 Uncertain.
K 18110 Uncertain.
K 18111 (+)K 4547+, Urgud, dup. *MSL* VII 113 117-120.
K 18112 Omens.
K 18113 Uncertain.
K 18114 Royal inscription of Ashurbanipal, dup. *VAB* VII p. 96 58-70.
K 18115 +K 9587 (*JNES* 33 341f.), Šimmatu incantations.
K 18116 Bilingual proverbs?
K 18117 +K 3455+, see K 17525.
K 18118 Large, coarse script.
K 18119 Religious, Sumerian?
K 18120 Bab. Religious/literary?
K 18121 +K 4900+, *CT* 17 38-39, see K 17627.
K 18122 Ritual?
K 18123 Uncertain.
K 18124 +K 4858, bilingual litany, dup. Sm 356 (*CLAM* p. 623).
K 18125 Bilingual.
K 18126 Bab.
K 18127 Maqlû V 43-49.
K 18128 Magico-medical.
K 18129 Queen of Nippur, Festschrift F. R. Kraus p. 180*.
K 18130 Uncertain.
K 18131 Uncertain.

K 18132 Bilingual.
K 18133 Bilingual.
K 18134 Uncertain.
K 18135 Uncertain.
K 18136 "*alkakāt ramkūti*".
K 18137 Uncertain.
K 18138 Uncertain.
K 18139 Sumerian?
K 18140 Bab.
K 18141 Uncertain.
K 18142 Medical?
K 18143 Literary/religious.
K 18144 Bilingual.
K 18145 Extispicy.
K 18146 Sequence of months.
K 18147 Neo-Assyrian administrative.
K 18148 Omens?
K 18149 Omens.
K 18150 Omens?
K 18151 +K 2725+, *RA* 17 125-6. Bilingual exorcism, ed. R. Borger, *AOAT* 1 1ff. See K 17168.
K 18152 Uncertain.
K 18153 Royal inscription?
K 18154 Library text.
K 18155 Omens.
K 18156 Omens.
K 18157 Sumerian, magic.
K 18158 Uncertain.
K 18159 Omens.
K 18160 +K 4555+, see K 17247, Nabnītu XVII 171-182 (*MSL* XVI 159).
K 18161 +K 13307, *JCS* 21 132, training of *bārû*-priest.
K 18162 Bab.
K 18163 Administrative record?
K 18164 Hymn/prayer.
K 18165 Omens?
K 18166 Uncertain.
K 18167 Uncertain.
K 18168 +K 3890+, Šurpu VIII 53-58, see K 17045.
K 18169 Uncertain.
K 18170 Uncertain.
K 18171 Omens or medical.
K 18172 Uncertain.
K 18173 Sumerian?
K 18174 Sumerian?
K 18175 Bilingual.
K 18176 Administrative record.
K 18177 List of names of Ea?
K 18178 "diš na *ina* ...".
K 18179 Cultic?
K 18180 Literary/religious?
K 18181 Omens.
K 18182 Omens?
K 18183 Gilgameš IX 142-148.
K 18184 Literary/religious.
K 18185 Religious?
K 18186 +K 3323+, Ludlul II 107-110.
K 18187 Religious/literary.
K 18188 Literary/religious.
K 18189 Uncertain.
K 18190 An=Anum III 132-147.
K 18191 +K 4596, Lú=ša, *MSL* XII 109 171-177.
K 18192 Uncertain.
K 18193 Lexical.
K 18194 Administrative?
K 18195 Uncertain.
K 18196 List of Akkadian words for "temple", cf. Malku=šarru I 255-265 (*JAOS* 83 429): to Aa?
K 18197 Medical/magic.
K 18198 Uncertain.
K 18199 Emesal.
K 18200 Uncertain.
K 18201 Ritual?
K 18202 Religious.
K 18203 Magico-medical.
K 18204 Uncertain.
K 18205 Bab. Ritual.
K 18206 Exorcistic.
K 18207 Omens?
K 18208 Šuilla?
K 18209 Bab. Sumerian?

K 18210 Sumerian proverbs.
K 18211 (+)K 4077, bilingual incantations, dup. Reiner, *Šurpu* p. 53. Cf. K 20555.
K 18212 Omens.
K 18213 Uncertain.
K 18214 Literary?
K 18215 Administrative?
K 18216 +K 4345+ (*CT* 14 25) obv. i-ii, plant list.
K 18217 Uncertain.
K 18218 Uncertain.
K 18219 Neo-Assyrian royal inscription ("king of Elam")?
K 18220 Uncertain.
K 18221 Uncertain.
K 18222 +K 4863+ (*CT* 16 31), Udugḫul VI 70-73.
K 18223 Bilingual?
K 18224 Administrative document?
K 18225 Literary/religious.
K 18226 Literary/religious. "*uštarriḫu sapāḫša*".
K 18227 Omens.
K 18228 Uncertain.
K 18229 Bab.
K 18230 Neo-Assyrian royal inscription?
K 18231 Omens.
K 18232 Uncertain.
K 18233 Omens.
K 18234 +K 4140a+, Köcher, *Pflanzen*, 16, plant list.
K 18235 +K 7027+, Tamītu.
K 18236 +K 8191+, Šumma ālu LXI A, *CT* 39 19 126-129.
K 18237 Ritual?
K 18238 Omens?
K 18239 Uncertain.
K 18240 Large, coarse script.
K 18241 Bilingual.
K 18242 Hymn.
K 18243 Uncertain.
K 18244 Omens.
K 18245 Uncertain.
K 18246 Omens.
K 18247 Uncertain.
K 18248 Prayer?
K 18249 Omens?
K 18250 Sons of Enmešarra.
K 18251 Bab. Ritual?
K 18252 Omens.
K 18253 Enūma Anu Enlil LXIV, cf. K 2568+.
K 18254 Ritual.
K 18255 Administrative?
K 18256 Omens?
K 18257 Uncertain.
K 18258 Gula Šuilla, dup. *AGH* p. 30 4-8, *UFBG* p. 455f. 12-16. See K 16864+.
K 18259 Medical prescriptions.
K 18260 Lexical.
K 18261 Neo-Assyrian royal inscription.
K 18262 Uncertain.
K 18263 Bab. List of professional titles.
K 18264 Colophon.
K 18265 Large, coarse script.
K 18266 Lexical.
K 18267 "*imittīšu u šumēlīšu*".
K 18268 Uncertain.
K 18269 Begins: "diš ud.ná.àm".
K 18270 Uncertain.
K 18271 Uncertain.
K 18272 Bab.
K 18273 Uncertain.
K 18274 Uncertain.
K 18275 Litany?
K 18276 Uncertain.
K 18277 Uncertain.
K 18278 Uncertain.
K 18279 Omens.
K 18280 Uncertain.
K 18281 Omens.
K 18282 Uncertain.
K 18283 Historical epic?
K 18284 Omens?
K 18285 +K 16864, which see.
K 18286 Liver omens.

K 18287 Religious/literary.
K 18288 Uncertain.
K 18289 +K 10343+ (*TDP* pl. xi, pp. 54ff.), medical.
K 18290 Uncertain.
K 18291 Uncertain.
K 18292 Omens?
K 18293 Omens.
K 18294 Uncertain.
K 18295 Literary/religious.
K 18296 Medical(?) ritual.
K 18297 Letter?
K 18298 Medical.
K 18299 Uncertain.
K 18300 Omens?
K 18301 Omens.
K 18302 Omens about eclipses, cf. K 17087.
K 18303 Ritual?
K 18304 Sumerian?
K 18305 Uncertain.
K 18306 Uncertain.
K 18307 Uncertain.
K 18308 Uncertain.
K 18309 +K 3455+. See K 17525.
K 18310 Uncertain.
K 18311 Uncertain.
K 18312 Uncertain.
K 18313 Uncertain.
K 18314 Omens?
K 18315 Uncertain.
K 18316 Uncertain.
K 18317 Neo-Assyrian administrative, grant/census?
K 18318 From top of Sennacherib(?) prism.
K 18319 Uncertain.
K 18320 Medical or ritual.
K 18321 Literary/religious.
K 18322 "*arratu*".
K 18323 Royal inscription?
K 18324 Omens?
K 18325 Uncertain.
K 18326 Uncertain.
K 18327 Uncertain.
K 18328 Literary/religious.
K 18329 +K 2257+ (*CT* 16 10 IV = 16 50 iv), Udugḫul IV. Cf. K 19809, 20360.
K 18330 Bilingual.
K 18331 +K 14735, Ḫulbazizi 120-122.
K 18332 Uncertain.
K 18333 Omens.
K 18334 (+)K 5135+, Bīt rimki, House III, *JCS* 21 7 57-59.
K 18335 "*erēb šamši*".
K 18336 Omens.
K 18337 Uncertain.
K 18338 Uncertain.
K 18339 Uncertain.
K 18340 Similar to K 5766. Astrology?
K 18341 Literary/religious.
K 18342 Uncertain.
K 18343 Bab. Magico-medical.
K 18344 Uncertain.
K 18345 Bab.
K 18346 "é-sis[kur]".
K 18347 Uncertain.
K 18348 Names Ashur.
K 18349 Omens?
K 18350 Omens.
K 18351 Uncertain.
K 18352 Medical?
K 18353 Uncertain.
K 18354 Uncertain.
K 18355 Omens?
K 18356 Uncertain.
K 18357 Bilingual?
K 18358 Magico-medical.
K 18359 Tamītu?
K 18360 Lexical? Cf. K 18402.
K 18361 Omens.
K 18362 Uncertain.
K 18363 Medical.
K 18364 Incantation prayer.
K 18365 Uncertain.
K 18366 Omens.
K 18367 Medical?

K 18368 Uncertain.
K 18369 Omens?
K 18370 Uncertain.
K 18371 Uncertain.
K 18372 Omens.
K 18373 "[*ipa*]*šša*[*ḫ*]".
K 18374 Uncertain.
K 18375 Neo-Assyrian legal; witness list?
K 18376 Uncertain.
K 18377 Sumerian Eršaḫunga, Maul p. 135, pl. 11*.
K 18378 Bab. +K 148 (*ACh* Supp. Ištar 36), astrological omens.
K 18379 Uncertain.
K 18380 Uncertain.
K 18381 Uncertain.
K 18382 Sumerian?
K 18383 Bilingual.
K 18384 Exorcism?
K 18385 Omens.
K 18386 Uncertain.
K 18387 Omens.
K 18388 Omens.
K 18389 Omens.
K 18390 Omens from winds.
K 18391 Bilingual.
K 18392 Medical.
K 18393 Uncertain.
K 18394 Uncertain.
K 18395 "*muššul*".
K 18396 Uncertain.
K 18397 Dup. Marduk prayer no. 2 (*AfO* 19 65), col. iv.
K 18398 Religious.
K 18399 Apotropaic?
K 18400 Uncertain.
K 18401 Uncertain.
K 18402 Similar to K 18360.
K 18403 Prayer, cf. *KAR* 292 obv.
K 18404 Uncertain.
K 18405 Uncertain.
K 18406 Sumerian or ritual.
K 18407 +K 3520 (*Babyloniaca* 6 127-128) obv. 1-6; dup. 80-7-19, 97.
K 18408 Literary/religious.
K 18409 Omens?
K 18410 Omens.
K 18411 Uncertain.
K 18412 Astrology.
K 18413 Uncertain.
K 18414 Uncertain.
K 18415 Medical.
K 18416 Uncertain.
K 18417 Bilingual.
K 18418 Šurpu III 179-184 and IV 1.
K 18419 Maqlû-type ritual and incantation.
K 18420 Omens.
K 18421 Literary/religious?
K 18422 Ritual and incantations?
K 18423 Listing of days of the month?
K 18424 Medical.
K 18425 Literary/religious.
K 18426 Omens?
K 18427 Uncertain.
K 18428 Large, coarse script. Administrative.
K 18429 Uncertain.
K 18430 Uncertain.
K 18431 Sumerian; repeated za.e.
K 18432 Uncertain.
K 18433 Ritual/omens?
K 18434 Literary.
K 18435 Uncertain.
K 18436 (+)K 10182+ etc. (M. Lebeau and P. Talon, eds., *Reflets des deux fleuves* (Akkadica Supplementum VI; Leuven, 1989) p. 95), catalogue.
K 18437 Meteorological omens.
K 18438 Related to Tintir=Bābilu II 21-24.
K 18439 Uncertain.
K 18440 +K 3455+. See K 17525.
K 18441 Uncertain.
K 18442 Omens?
K 18443 Uncertain.
K 18444 Uncertain.

K 18445 Medical or other recipe.
K 18446 Omens.
K 18447 "[*bu-u*]*p-pa-ni*-[x]".
K 18448 +K 19299 (+)K 5034, dup. Sm 504. Sumerian incantation.
K 18449 Uncertain.
K 18450 (+)K 3587, work songs, *ZA* 70 55*.
K 18451 Bab. Uncertain.
K 18452 Snake omens.
K 18453 Uncertain.
K 18454 Uncertain.
K 18455 Uncertain.
K 18456 Uncertain.
K 18457 Uncertain.
K 18458 Omens and Nabû-zuqup-kēna colophon.
K 18459 Erra myth?
K 18460 Extispicy?
K 18461 Literary/religious.
K 18462 Omens?
K 18463 +K 10275, Tamītu.
K 18464 Omens.
K 18465 Omens.
K 18466 Omens?
K 18467 +K 4555+, see K 17247.
K 18468 Omens?
K 18469 Large, coarse Bab.
K 18470 Tamītu?
K 18471 Prayer?
K 18472 Ritual?
K 18473 Uncertain.
K 18474 Neo-Assyrian letter.
K 18475 Literary/religious.
K 18476 Large, coarse script.
K 18477 Lines ending "*šalmat*/*salmat*".
K 18478 Neo-Assyrian letter.
K 18479 +K 3399+, Atra-ḫasīs I (*AfO* 27 74*).
K 18480 Uncertain.
K 18481 Bab.
K 18482 +K 2413 (*AMT* 67 1), dup. *BAM* 248 iii 7-12, medical.
K 18483 Uncertain.
K 18484 Omens.
K 18485 Concerning attacks of demons.
K 18486 Bab. Lexical?
K 18487 Uncertain.
K 18488 +K 3349+, Marduk's Address. See K 17113.
K 18489 +K 17138, which see.
K 18490 (+)K 203+, instructions for glass-making, see K 20141.
K 18491 Uncertain.
K 18492 Large, coarse Bab.
K 18493 Uncertain.
K 18494 Uncertain.
K 18495 Uncertain.
K 18496 Omens?
K 18497 Omens.
K 18498 Uncertain.
K 18499 Uncertain.
K 18500 Religious?
K 18501 +K 5046+, cf. Udugḫul IX 97-103.
K 18502 Uncertain.
K 18503 Bab.
K 18504 Bilingual in parallel columns.
K 18505 Uncertain.
K 18506 Literary/religious.
K 18507 Prism fragment.
K 18508 Uncertain.
K 18509 Uncertain.
K 18510 +K 2148+ (*MIO* 1 57ff.), Göttertypentext.
K 18511 Literary.
K 18512 Uncertain.
K 18513 Exorcistic.
K 18514 Neo-Assyrian letter?
K 18515 Uncertain.
K 18516 Uncertain.
K 18517 Omens.
K 18518 Uncertain.
K 18519 Uncertain.
K 18520 Uncertain.
K 18521 Uncertain.
K 18522 Sumerian?
K 18523 Uncertain.

K 18524 Bilingual?
K 18525 Administrative.
K 18526 Uncertain.
K 18527 Uncertain.
K 18528 Uncertain.
K 18529 Prayer?
K 18530 Bab.
K 18531 Tamītu, (+)K 2383?
K 18532 Omens.
K 18533 Letter to Kurig[alzu]?
K 18534 Erra I 151-156, *AfO* 27 77*.
K 18535 Theodicy 254-259.
K 18536 "*taḫ-l*[*u-up-tu, sis-si*[*k-tu*".
K 18537 Uncertain.
K 18538 +K 2578+ (*CT* 16 10 iv 24-27), Udugḫul IV.
K 18539 Incantation?
K 18540 Omens.
K 18541 +K 9728+ (Johns, *Doomsday Book* pl. 13).
K 18542 Uncertain.
K 18543 Uncertain.
K 18544 Bilingual religious, cf. K 2893+ (Gattung II)?
K 18545 Lexical?
K 18546 Bab. Uncertain.
K 18547 Bab. (+)K 8716 (*AMT* 54 3), medical.
K 18548 Uncertain.
K 18549 Uncertain.
K 18550 Uncertain.
K 18551 Uncertain.
K 18552 Dup. K 2485+ (*BL* 71) obv. 58-62, Sumerian litany, see *ASJ* 7 27, 278-282; (+)K 11857.
K 18553 Middle Assyrian script.
K 18554 Administrative.
K 18555 Omens?
K 18556 Bab. "*i-ḫa-al*".
K 18557 Omens.
K 18558 "*tur-tum*".
K 18559 Omens.
K 18560 Omens?
K 18561 Ashurbanipal colophon.
K 18562 Omens.
K 18563 Uncertain.
K 18564 List of Ištar names?
K 18565 Prism fragment.
K 18566 Omens?
K 18567 Uncertain.
K 18568 Uncertain.
K 18569 Omens?
K 18570 Astrology?
K 18571 Uncertain.
K 18572 +K 3399+, Atra-ḫasīs I (*AfO* 27 72*). See K 21851.
K 18573 Administrative?
K 18574 Uncertain.
K 18575 Uncertain.
K 18576 Enūma eliš VII 124-127.
K 18577 Uncertain.
K 18578 Uncertain.
K 18579 Uncertain.
K 18580 Sumerian.
K 18581 Omens.
K 18582 Omens.
K 18583 Prism fragment.
K 18584 Uncertain.
K 18585 Scholarly text.
K 18586 Uncertain.
K 18587 (+)K 6488 (*AMT* 85 1)? Medical.
K 18588 Uncertain.
K 18589 Administrative?
K 18590 Bab. Omens.
K 18591 Bab. Ritual involving brick-mould and well.
K 18592 Bab.
K 18593 Bab. Omens?
K 18594 Medical.
K 18595 Bab.
K 18596 Omens.
K 18597 Bab. Bilingual.
K 18598 Bab.
K 18599 Bab.
K 18600 Bab. Grammatical list?
K 18601 +K 2290+ (*BAM* 543), medical.
K 18602 Neo-Assyrian royal inscription?

K 18603 Bilingual royal inscription, Cassite or II Isin?
K 18604 Uncertain.
K 18605 "níg.sag.íl.la".
K 18606 Omens.
K 18607 Bilingual.
K 18608 Bab. Omens.
K 18609 Bab. Maqlû III 100-107.
K 18610 Neo-Babylonian letter.
K 18611 Small Bab.
K 18612 (+)K 2947+, (+)K 7561+, Maqlû II 89-96.
K 18613 Bab. Omens?
K 18614 Coarse script.
K 18615 Lamaštu?
K 18616 Concerns amulet-stones.
K 18617 Marduk's Address.
K 18618 Maqlû-type incantation.
K 18619 Uncertain.
K 18620 Literary/religious.
K 18621 Omens.
K 18622 Medical?
K 18623 Large, coarse Bab.
K 18624 Large Bab.
K 18625 Bab. Religious?
K 18626 +K 2427+, Šurpu IX 1-8.
K 18627 Bab.
K 18628 Bab. Literary/religious. Bilingual?
K 18629 Large Bab.
K 18630 Bab. Magic/religious.
K 18631 Bab.
K 18632 "*eṭlu u ardatu*".
K 18633 +K 2866+, Šurpu VIII 28-33.
K 18634 Old Babylonian fragment.
K 18635 Omens.
K 18636 Bab. Ritual.
K 18637 Bab. Bilingual?
K 18638 Neo-Assyrian administrative.
K 18639 Bab. Bilingual.
K 18640 Omens.
K 18641 Uncertain.
K 18642 Medical?
K 18643 +K 5007+...20375+21383 +21384, bilingual litany, A'abba ḫuluḫḫa (*CLAM* pp. 384ff). Cf. K 17640, K 17657 and K 18669.
K 18644 "*tapaqqid*".
K 18645 Bab. Hemerology.
K 18646 Bab.
K 18647 Sumerian?
K 18648 Bilingual.
K 18649 Neo-Assyrian oracle question, *SAA* IV 127*.
K 18650 Omens?
K 18651 +K 5337+, see K 17424.
K 18652 Ashurbanipal colophon.
K 18653 Bab. Literary/religious.
K 18654 Bab. Sumerian?
K 18655 Bab. (+)K 5174+, dup. K 5168+, K 17891 (+)Rm 272. See Cohen, *Eršemma* p. 125.
K 18656 Bab. Astrology?
K 18657 Bab.
K 18658 Bab. Ritual/omens?
K 18659 Uncertain.
K 18660 Bab. Omens with colophon.
K 18661 Bab.
K 18662 Omens or list?
K 18663 Bab. Bilingual?
K 18664 Lexical?
K 18665 Bab. Bilingual.
K 18666 Literary or royal inscription.
K 18667 Bab. Medical.
K 18668 Bilingual?
K 18669 +K 4981+, bilingual litany, A'abba ḫuluḫḫa (*CLAM* pp. 384ff.). Cf. K 18643.
K 18670 Omens.
K 18671 Coarse script, round(?) tablet.
K 18672 Literary/religious.
K 18673 Ritual or incantation?
K 18674 Love lyrics?
K 18675 Omens.
K 18676 Bab. Omens.
K 18677 Bab. Literary/religious.

K 18678 Bilingual.
K 18679 Bab. Religious.
K 18680 Bab. Bilingual.
K 18681 Ritual. Cf. K 13406.
K 18682 Uncertain.
K 18683 Bab. Ritual?
K 18684 Bilingual prayer.
K 18685 Omens.
K 18686 Bab.
K 18687 Uncertain.
K 18688 Bab. Omens?
K 18689 Bab. Astrology?
K 18690 Ritual?
K 18691 Medical.
K 18692 Uncertain.
K 18693 List?
K 18694 +K 4928 (+)K2451, Mīs pî V.
K 18695 Bab. Ritual, Maul p. 52, pl. 2*.
K 18696 Sumerian?
K 18697 Bab.
K 18698 Bab.
K 18699 Bab. Hymn?
K 18700 Omens.
K 18701 Uncertain.
K 18702 Literary?
K 18703 Mentions together "*muṣri ḫatti*".
K 18704 Uncertain.
K 18705 Uncertain.
K 18706 Bab.
K 18707 Bab.
K 18708 Bab. Omens?
K 18709 Uncertain.
K 18710 +K 4424+, Urra=ḫubullu IV 196-199 (*MSL* V 168).
K 18711 Bab. +K 8733, dup. K 5222+, bilingual Eršaḫunga, Maul p. 366-367, pl. 59* Cf. K 5168+.
K 18712 Sumerian.
K 18713 Iqqur īpuš or hemerology?
K 18714 Omens.
K 18715 Uncertain.
K 18716 Literary/religious.
K 18717 Omens?
K 18718 Bab.
K 18719 Bab. Prayer?
K 18720 Omens? Medical?
K 18721 Uncertain.
K 18722 Bab. Dup. *ACh* Supp. Ištar XXXIII 46-52 (K 137), astrological omens.
K 18723 Uncertain.
K 18724 Bab. Emesal litany.
K 18725 +Sm 1361, Emesal litany, dup. *CLAM* p. 211.
K 18726 Bab. Sumerian litany, Maul p. 337, pl. 53*.
K 18727 Bab. Literary/religious.
K 18728 Bab. Astrological omens.
K 18729 Uncertain.
K 18730 Bab. Religious?
K 18731 Bab. Omens?
K 18732 Bilingual litany, cf. *SBH* p. 100 8-12 = *CLAM* p. 714 195-197.
K 18733 Bab. Astrological omens.
K 18734 Bab.
K 18735 Uncertain.
K 18736 Bab. Bilingual litany.
K 18737 Omens.
K 18738 Astrological omens.
K 18739 Coarse Bab. Letter?
K 18740 Bab. Anzû II 59-64 or 74-79 (*AfO* 27 82*), (+)K 3008 (+)K 19368 (+)K 21072.
K 18741 Omens.
K 18742 Bab. Literary/religious?
K 18743 +K 5364+, dup. K 5992, Sumerian/bilingual Eršaḫunga, Maul p. 97, pl. 9*. See K 19092.
K 18744 Names Emelamanna.
K 18745 Bab. Ritual?
K 18746 Omens or ritual?
K 18747 Sumerian.
K 18748 Sumerian.
K 18749 Bab. Literary/religious?
K 18750 Bab. Omens.
K 18751 Bab. Omens.
K 18752 Bab.

K 18753 Middle Assyrian script. Omens.
K 18754 Uncertain.
K 18755 (+)81-2-4, 410b, dup. *CT* 16 20 65-72, Udugḫul XVI.
K 18756 Bab. Letter?
K 18757 Bab. Literary/religious.
K 18758 Bab.
K 18759 Bab.
K 18760 Bab.
K 18761 Bab. Religious?
K 18762 Bab. Medical.
K 18763 Omens.
K 18764 Bab. Omens.
K 18765 Uncertain.
K 18766 Bab. Omens.
K 18767 Bab. Letter?
K 18768 Bab.
K 18769 Literary/religious.
K 18770 Bab. Omens.
K 18771 "Stars".
K 18772 Late Babylonian economic, cf. K 4790, 10197+19134, 19164, 19307, 19693, 20190.
K 18773 Bab. Cure for scorpion bite?
K 18774 Bab. Literary/religious.
K 18775 Bab. Omens?
K 18776 Bab.
K 18777 Bab. Omens.
K 18778 Cf. Šurpu?
K 18779 Bab. Omens.
K 18780 Bab. Ritual.
K 18781 +K 5119+ (*JRAS* 1935 459ff., see *Or*. NS 30 1ff.), Bīt mēseri III.
K 18782 Bab. Sumerian?
K 18783 Bab. Literary/religious?
K 18784 Bab. Literary.
K 18785 Bab.
K 18786 Uncertain.
K 18787 Bab. Bilingual.
K 18788 Letter?
K 18789 Bab.
K 18790 Bab. Extispicy?
K 18791 +K 14818 (*CLAM* pp. 23, 829*), incipits of litanies, note: "im-ma-al gù-d[é-dé]".
K 18792 +K 2866+, Šurpu VIII 88-90 and IX 1.
K 18793 Sumerian?
K 18794 Bab. Bilingual litany, cf. K 5587.
K 18795 Bab.
K 18796 Coarse Bab.
K 18797 Bab. Literary/religious.
K 18798 Omens.
K 18799 Omens?
K 18800 Bab.
K 18801 Omens (liver?).
K 18802 Literary/religious.
K 18803 Literary/religious.
K 18804 Uncertain.
K 18805 Literary.
K 18806 Uncertain.
K 18807 +K 2856+, bottom of obv. i, (*AJSL* 35 136-137), Mīs pî.
K 18808 Astrological omens.
K 18809 Omens?
K 18810 +K 2079+ (*ACh* Sin XIII), dup. Sm 1171 (*CT* 26 46) rev., astronomy.
K 18811 Bab.
K 18812 Uncertain.
K 18813 Dup. *VAB* VII pp. 76-78 64-70, Ashurbanipal royal inscription.
K 18814 Bab.
K 18815 +K 5096+ (*CT* 16 14 iii 57-iv 2), Udugḫul V.
K 18816 Omens(?) about answering (*apālu*).
K 18817 Uncertain.
K 18818 Literary/religious?
K 18819 +K 2001+ (Farber, *Ištar und Dumuzi* p. 130 61-65, pl. 9), incantation.
K 18820 Uncertain.
K 18821 Uncertain.
K 18822 Ritual.

K 18823 Uncertain.
K 18824 Omens.
K 18825 Omens or ritual?
K 18826 Literary/religious.
K 18827 Bilingual.
K 18828 Uncertain.
K 18829 Literary/religious.
K 18830 Bilingual?
K 18831 Omens.
K 18832 Ritual or omens?
K 18833 Uncertain.
K 18834 +K 13857, Marduk's Address.
K 18835 +K 9968+ (Wiggermann, *BPF* pp. 11; 24-26 105-116; 340-341*), making of images.
K 18836 Ritual.
K 18837 Bilingual Eršaḫunga, Maul p. 296 15-18, pl. 45*.
K 18838 Omens.
K 18839 Uncertain.
K 18840 Omens.
K 18841 Omens.
K 18842 Uncertain.
K 18843 Letter?
K 18844 Small Bab. script. Namburbi.
K 18845 Literary/religious.
K 18846 Uncertain.
K 18847 Uncertain.
K 18848 Ashurbanipal colophon.
K 18849 Omens?
K 18850 Bab. Literary?
K 18851 Bilingual.
K 18852 Omens.
K 18853 Sumerian.
K 18854 Uncertain.
K 18855 Bilingual?
K 18856 Uncertain.
K 18857 Omens?
K 18858 Uncertain.
K 18859 Omens.
K 18860 Literary/religious ((*me*)*rêti u mašqīti*).
K 18861 Uncertain.
K 18862 Uncertain.
K 18863 Literary/religious.
K 18864 +K 2109+, see K 16880.
K 18865 Omens.
K 18866 Uncertain.
K 18867 Uncertain.
K 18868 Bab. Omens?
K 18869 Emesal litany.
K 18870 Uncertain.
K 18871 Bab. Ritual?
K 18872 Uncertain.
K 18873 List?
K 18874 Uncertain.
K 18875 Bab.
K 18876 Uncertain.
K 18877 Bab. Small oblong tablet.
K 18878 Sumerian?
K 18879 Omens.
K 18880 Uncertain.
K 18881 Uncertain.
K 18882 Omens?
K 18883 Omens.
K 18884 Bilingual litany?
K 18885 Omens.
K 18886 Uncertain.
K 18887 Bab.
K 18888 Bab. +K 2937+ (*CT* 40 30), Šumma ālu XL.
K 18889 Coarse Bab.?
K 18890 Literary/religious?
K 18891 Uncertain.
K 18892 Uncertain.
K 18893 Uncertain.
K 18894 Uncertain.
K 18895 Literary/religious?
K 18896 Letter?
K 18897 Colophon.
K 18898 Bab. Uncertain.
K 18899 Bilingual, cf. K 20011.
K 18900 Uncertain.
K 18901 Bab. Ritual?
K 18902 Omens.
K 18903 Literary/religious.
K 18904 Temple names.
K 18905 Uncertain.

K 18906 Uncertain.
K 18907 Uncertain.
K 18908 Literary/religious.
K 18909 Liver omens.
K 18910 Omens.
K 18911 Uncertain.
K 18912 Uncertain.
K 18913 Omens.
K 18914 Sumerian litany? Cf. *CLAM* p. 190.
K 18915 Omens?
K 18916 Omens.
K 18917 Bilingual incantation (Marduk-Ea type).
K 18918 Bab.
K 18919 Royal inscription?
K 18920 Uncertain.
K 18921 Omens.
K 18922 Uncertain.
K 18923 Uncertain.
K 18924 Uncertain.
K 18925 Dup. *SBH* p. 130 5-11, see J. A. Black, *BiOr* 44 40, no. 6.
K 18926 Omens.
K 18927 Uncertain.
K 18928 +K 17251, which see.
K 18929 Uncertain.
K 18930 Bilingual?
K 18931 Catch-line of hymn?
K 18932 Tamītu?
K 18933 Bab.
K 18934 Omens.
K 18935 Uncertain.
K 18936 Omens.
K 18937 Omens.
K 18938 Omens?
K 18939 Uncertain.
K 18940 Uncertain.
K 18941 Bilingual?
K 18942 Coarse Bab.
K 18943 Ritual?
K 18944 Omens?
K 18945 Uncertain.
K 18946 Uncertain.
K 18947 "*šangammaḫu*".
K 18948 Uncertain.
K 18949 Uncertain.
K 18950 Liver omens?
K 18951 Sumerian?
K 18952 Uncertain.
K 18953 Omens?
K 18954 Uncertain.
K 18955 Coarse script.
K 18956 Antagal F 241-246 (*MSL* 17 219*).
K 18957 Coarse script.
K 18958 Uncertain.
K 18959 Literary/religious.
K 18960 Bab. Ritual?
K 18961 Omens.
K 18962 Bab. Omens.
K 18963 +K 1757, Ludlul I 51-55.
K 18964 Omens.
K 18965 Uncertain
K 18966 Omens.
K 18967 Bab. Historiography?
K 18968 Uncertain.
K 18969 Uncertain.
K 18970 Bab. Omens?
K 18971 Bab. Literary/religious?
K 18972 Uncertain.
K 18973 Uncertain.
K 18974 Bab. Prayer?
K 18975 Library text.
K 18976 Bab. Letter(?) mentioning "kur.*a-ra-ši* ".
K 18977 Medical.
K 18978 Omens?
K 18979 Bab. Prayer or literary?
K 18980 Bab.
K 18981 Bab.
K 18982 Bab.
K 18983 (+)K 8787+ (*ADD* 1110+), Neo-Assyrian administrative. See K 20414.
K 18984 Bab. Omens?
K 18985 Bab. Ritual?
K 18986 Uncertain.

K 18987 Bab. Omens?
K 18988 Bab.
K 18989 Bab. Omens?
K 18990 Bab. Omens?
K 18991 Bab.
K 18992 Bab. Incantation.
K 18993 Bab. Omens?
K 18994 Bab.
K 18995 Bab. Omens.
K 18996 Bab. Ritual.
K 18997 Bab.
K 18998 Ritual.
K 18999 Bab. Omens.
K 19000 Uncertain.
K 19001 Literary/religious.
K 19002 Bab. Omens?
K 19003 Bab. Bilingual?
K 19004 Uncertain.
K 19005 Bab. Library text.
K 19006 Omens.
K 19007 Library records, cf. *JNES* 42 1-29.
K 19008 Prayers?
K 19009 Bab. Prayers?
K 19010 Bab. Omens?
K 19011 Uncertain.
K 19012 Bab. Colophon?
K 19013 Neo-Assyrian administrative.
K 19014 Bab.
K 19015 Bab.
K 19016 Exorcism (*šār bērī*)?
K 19017 Bab. Omens.
K 19018 Coarse Bab.
K 19019 Bab. +K 2342+ rev. 4-12 (*ACh* Ištar XXI), astrological omens.
K 19020 Bab.
K 19021 Bab. Literary/religious.
K 19022 Bab. Omens.
K 19023 Bab. Literary/religious?
K 19024 Bab. Lexical.
K 19025 Bab.
K 19026 Bab. Omens.
K 19027 Royal inscription?
K 19028 Bab. Omens?
K 19029 Bab. Colophon ("tablet of Adad-MU-[").
K 19030 Uncertain.
K 19031 Library tablet.
K 19032 Archaizing script?
K 19033 Bab. Literary/religious.
K 19034 Bab.
K 19035 Large, coarse Bab.
K 19036 Literary/religious.
K 19037 Bab. (+)(?)K 19350, which see.
K 19038 Bab.
K 19039 Bab.
K 19040 Omens.
K 19041 Bab. Bilingual?
K 19042 Omens.
K 19043 Bab.
K 19044 Bab. Ritual and incantation/hymn/prayer.
K 19045 Omens.
K 19046 Bab.
K 19047 Coarse Bab.
K 19048 Coarse Bab.
K 19049 Neo-Assyrian royal inscription?
K 19050 Literary/religious.
K 19051 Uncertain.
K 19052 Bab. Hymn to Eru'a.
K 19053 Bab. Liver omens.
K 19054 Omens.
K 19055 Bab.
K 19056 Bab. Namburbi?
K 19057 Bab. Exorcism or extispicy?
K 19058 Omens.
K 19059 Sumerian?
K 19060 Large script. Mentions Ashurbanipal.
K 19061 Bab. Iqqur īpuš.
K 19062 Bab. Magic or medical.
K 19063 Bab. Omens(?) and colophon mentioning Amēl-Gula.
K 19064 Uncertain.
K 19065 Bab.
K 19066 Dup. *KAR* 80 rev. 6-13, incantation prayer, see *UFBG* 417 52.

K 19067 Bab. Literary/religious.
K 19068 Neo-Assyrian royal inscription.
K 19069 Bilingual.
K 19070 Bab. Omens?
K 19071 Bab.
K 19072 Bab. Omens?
K 19073 Large Bab.
K 19074 Uncertain.
K 19075 Bab. Omens?
K 19076 Bab.
K 19077 Bab. Neo-Assyrian oracle question, *SAA* IV 230*.
K 19078 Bab. Omens.
K 19079 Omens.
K 19080 Bab.
K 19081 Large Middle Assyrian script. Royal inscription?
K 19082 Bab.
K 19083 Selected days of the month listed.
K 19084 Bab. Omens?
K 19085 Bab. Omens.
K 19086 Bab. Omens.
K 19087 Medical?
K 19088 Omens.
K 19089 Bab. Litany.
K 19090 (+)K 8787+ (*ADD* 1110+), Neo-Assyrian administrative.
K 19091 Bab. Omens.
K 19092 Bab. +K 5364+ obv., see K 18743.
K 19093 Uncertain.
K 19094 Uncertain.
K 19095 Bab. Literary/religious.
K 19096 Bab.
K 19097 Bab. Literary/religious.
K 19098 Tamītu.
K 19099 Omens.
K 19100 Bab. Omens.
K 19101 Bab. Ritual of Esagil, (+)(?)K 8742, K 8878, 81-7-27, 129.
K 19102 Bab. Omens.
K 19103 Uncertain.
K 19104 Uncertain.
K 19105 Uncertain.
K 19106 Ritual.
K 19107 Omens?
K 19108 Bab. Literary?
K 19109 Omens?
K 19110 Bab. Uncertain.
K 19111 Uncertain.
K 19112 Bab.
K 19113 Bab. Dup. *KAR* 161, bilingual Eršaḫunga, Maul p. 73, pl. 7*.
K 19114 Bab. Omens?
K 19115 Magical stones?
K 19116 Bab. Literary/religious.
K 19117 Middle Assyrian?
K 19118 Bilingual Eršaḫunga, Maul p. 374, pl. 61*.
K 19119 Uncertain.
K 19120 Omens?
K 19121 Omens?
K 19122 Uncertain.
K 19123 "Wall … palace".
K 19124 Uncertain.
K 19125 Bab.
K 19126 Religious.
K 19127 Neo-Assyrian administrative?
K 19128 Literary/religious.
K 19129 Uncertain.
K 19130 Omens.
K 19131 Medical?
K 19132 Bab. Ritual.
K 19133 Large Bab. Sumerian?
K 19134 +K 10197, Late Babylonian administrative. See K 18772.
K 19135 Omens.
K 19136 Omens with commentary?
K 19137 Bab. Omens.
K 19138 Bab. Omens.
K 19139 Sumerian catch-line?
K 19140 Bab.
K 19141 Uncertain.
K 19142 Bab. Omens.
K 19143 Omens about Sargon of Akkad.
K 19144 Uncertain.
K 19145 Uncertain.

K 19146 Uncertain.
K 19147 "82-5-22". Neo-Assyrian letter, *SAA* I no. 73 and p. 255*.
K 19148 Bab. Uncertain.
K 19149 Uncertain.
K 19150 Bab.
K 19151 Letter?
K 19152 Uncertain.
K 19153 Uncertain.
K 19154 Bab. Maqlû-type incantations.
K 19155 Omens.
K 19156 Uncertain.
K 19157 Bab.
K 19158 Literary/religious.
K 19159 Literary/religious.
K 19160 Sumerian litany.
K 19161 Colophon.
K 19162 Neo-Assyrian administrative.
K 19163 Religious?
K 19164 Late Babylonian administrative, see K 18772.
K 19165 Omens.
K 19166 Sloping Bab.
K 19167 Bab.
K 19168 Sumerian?
K 19169 Ritual?
K 19170 Uncertain.
K 19171 Bilingual?
K 19172 Omens?
K 19173 Omens?
K 19174 Neo-Assyrian administrative?
K 19175 Bab.
K 19176 Religious?
K 19177 Omens or ritual?
K 19178 Incantation?
K 19179 Ritual?
K 19180 Bab. archaizing script.
K 19181 Omens.
K 19182 Bab.
K 19183 Uncertain.
K 19184 Uncertain.
K 19185 Uncertain.
K 19186 Bab.
K 19187 Dup. *CT* 39 22 1-3, Šumma ālu LXI.
K 19188 Medical.
K 19189 Bab. Omens.
K 19190 Bab. Omens.
K 19191 Omens.
K 19192 Bab. Mīs pî?
K 19193 Bab. Omens?
K 19194 Coarse script.
K 19195 +K 7469+, jewelry.
K 19196 Bab. Letter.
K 19197 Coarse Bab. Oracle question?
K 19198 Bab.
K 19199 Omens.
K 19200 Bab. Omens?
K 19201 Uncertain.
K 19202 Commentary?
K 19203 Omens?
K 19204 Uncertain.
K 19205 Literary/religious?
K 19206 Omens.
K 19207 Bilingual?
K 19208 Literary/religious.
K 19209 Bab. Omens.
K 19210 Bab. Bilingual.
K 19211 Legal/administrative?
K 19212 Bab. Omens.
K 19213 Uncertain.
K 19214 Bab. Omens.
K 19215 Hymn?
K 19216 Liver omens.
K 19217 Ritual?
K 19218 Bab. Omens. Cf. K 8744.
K 19219 Uncertain.
K 19220 Omens?
K 19221 Bab.
K 19222 Bab. Bilingual litany.
K 19223 Bab.
K 19224 Bab. Šumma izbu?
K 19225 Ritual.
K 19226 Bab.
K 19227 Bab. Omens.
K 19228 Uncertain.
K 19229 Omens.

K 19230 Uncertain.
K 19231 Omens.
K 19232 Library text.
K 19233 Lines ending KI+MIN.
K 19234 Uncertain.
K 19235 Bilingual?
K 19236 Literary?
K 19237 Uncertain.
K 19238 Uncertain.
K 19239 Neo-Assyrian royal inscription?
K 19240 Library tablet.
K 19241 +K 2333+, (+)K 13995, Šurpu IV.
K 19242 Uncertain.
K 19243 "*šalṭiš*".
K 19244 Ritual?
K 19245 Medical?
K 19246 Omens?
K 19247 "*ḫadîš*".
K 19248 Uncertain.
K 19249 Astrological.
K 19250 Uncertain.
K 19251 Omens.
K 19252 Omens.
K 19253 Uncertain.
K 19254 Neo-Assyrian administrative.
K 19255 "*kaššî … sutî*".
K 19256 Bab.
K 19257 +K 3586+ (*CT* 17 35 69-75) rev. 1-7, Alam-níg-sag-íl-la.
K 19258 Sumerian or bilingual.
K 19259 Omens.
K 19260 (+)K 3211+ (Oppenheim, *Glass* pp. 43-44 109-118), glass making.
K 19261 Uncertain.
K 19262 Omens?
K 19263 Uncertain.
K 19264 Bab.
K 19265 Uncertain.
K 19266 Colophon?
K 19267 Incantations.
K 19268 Uncertain.
K 19269 Ḫulbazizi 58-61 ((+)K 9022?).
K 19270 Uncertain.
K 19271 Bab. Medical.
K 19272 Uncertain.
K 19273 Bab.
K 19274 Bird omens, cf. *CT* 41 6-8.
K 19275 Uncertain.
K 19276 Uncertain.
K 19277 Bilingual litany, dup. *CLAM* pp. 441-442 24-27; see K 17424+.
K 19278 Uncertain.
K 19279 Bilingual.
K 19280 Bab. Colophon.
K 19281 Uncertain.
K 19282 Literary?
K 19283 Uncertain.
K 19284 Uncertain.
K 19285 Bilingual litany.
K 19286 Omens?
K 19287 Bab.
K 19288 Neo-Assyrian legal, conveyance.
K 19289 Bab.
K 19290 Neo-Assyrian administrative?
K 19291 Uncertain.
K 19292 Omens?
K 19293 Sumerian litany (cf. J. A. Black, *BiOr* 44 41 B7 and 50 B36).
K 19294 Uncertain.
K 19295 Bab. Prophecies?
K 19296 Bab. Omens?
K 19297 Bab. Omens?
K 19298 Uncertain.
K 19299 +K 18448, which see.
K 19300 Uncertain.
K 19301 Uncertain.
K 19302 Literary/religious.
K 19303 Bab.
K 19304 Bab. +K 7598+ (*CLAM* p. 571 282-285), bilingual litany.
K 19305 +K 258+, Šumma izbu I 76, 78, 82 (*TCS* 4 38-39).
K 19306 Omens.
K 19307 Late Babylonian administrative, cf. K 18772.
K 19308 Uncertain.

K 19309 Temple list, (+)K 4407+.
K 19310 Uncertain.
K 19311 Bilingual Eršaḫunga, Maul p. 369, pl. 60*.
K 19312 Uncertain.
K 19313 Literary.
K 19314 Medical?
K 19315 Neo-Assyrian administrative, textiles.
K 19316 Uncertain.
K 19317 Uncertain.
K 19318 Omens.
K 19319 Bab. Omens?
K 19320 Bab.
K 19321 Bab.
K 19322 Ashurbanipal colophon.
K 19323 Bab. Royal inscription?
K 19324 Uncertain.
K 19325 (+)K 8590, Gilgameš VII iii.
K 19326 +K 47+, Šumma ālu LXI 25-28 (*CT* 39 15), omens.
K 19327 Uncertain.
K 19328 Liver omens.
K 19329 Literary/religious.
K 19330 Bab. Omens.
K 19331 Bab. Omens.
K 19332 Bab.
K 19333 Bab.
K 19334 Uncertain.
K 19335 Sumerian?
K 19336 Uncertain.
K 19337 Bab. Religious?
K 19338 Omens?
K 19339 Bab.
K 19340 Uncertain.
K 19341 +K 3622, Bīt mēseri II 87-94 (*AfO* 14 144).
K 19342 Magic.
K 19343 Bab. Omens.
K 19344 Bab. Medical?
K 19345 Bab. Letter?
K 19346 Bab. Eršemma fragment, bilingual.
K 19347 Bab. Omens?
K 19348 Bab. Tamītu/Ikrib?
K 19349 Bab. Omens?
K 19350 Bab. (+)K 19037(?), dup. K 3045 (*ABL* 924), letter of Adadšumuṣur to Aššur-nīrāri and Nabû-dayyāni.
K 19351 Bab.
K 19352 Bab.
K 19353 Letter?
K 19354 Bab.
K 19355 Bab. Medical.
K 19356 Bab. Omens or medical.
K 19357 Namburbi or related.
K 19358 Uncertain.
K 19359 Bab. “Alammuš”.
K 19360 Letter?
K 19361 Bab. Omens?
K 19362 Bab.
K 19363 Uncertain.
K 19364 Bab. “*šar pūḫi*”.
K 19365 Bab. Omens.
K 19366 Omens.
K 19367 Bab. Prayer?
K 19368 Bab. Anzû II 89-92, *AfO* 27 82*, (+)K 3008 (+)K 18740 (+)K 21072.
K 19369 Bilingual.
K 19370 Treaty curses?
K 19371 Uncertain.
K 19372 Uncertain.
K 19373 Magic, ritual?
K 19374 Uncertain with colophon.
K 19375 Epilogue to Laws of Hammurabi (XLVIII 79-87), Borger, *BAL* 2 p. 50*.
K 19376 Bab.
K 19377 Bilingual?
K 19378 Bab. Medical or magic.
K 19379 +Sm 314, dup. *CT* 17 9 19-22, bilingual incantation.
K 19380 +K 5337+, see K 17424+.
K 19381 Bab.
K 19382 Omens?
K 19383 Uncertain.

K 19384 Uncertain.
K 19385 Omens.
K 19386 Royal inscription of Ashurbanipal.
K 19387 Bilingual litany.
K 19388 Uncertain.
K 19389 (+)K 19443 (+)K 19479 (which see), astrological omens.
K 19390 Bilingual.
K 19391 Literary.
K 19392 Bab.
K 19393 Uncertain.
K 19394 Diagnostic omens?
K 19395 Omens?
K 19396 Uncertain.
K 19397 Liver omens.
K 19398 Bab.
K 19399 Bab. Uncertain.
K 19400 Omens.
K 19401 +K 3018+ (*Iraq* 32 60 21-23), bilingual Marduk Šuilla.
K 19402 Bab.
K 19403 Uncertain.
K 19404 Diagnostic omens?
K 19405 Uncertain.
K 19406 Omens.
K 19407 Ritual and prayer to Marduk.
K 19408 Bilingual Emesal litany.
K 19409 Uncertain.
K 19410 Bab. Literary/religious.
K 19411 Omens.
K 19412 Bab. Omens.
K 19413 Uncertain.
K 19414 Uncertain.
K 19415 Omens?
K 19416 Uncertain.
K 19417 Administrative?
K 19418 Omens?
K 19419 Sumerian.
K 19420 Omens?
K 19421 Ashurbanipal prism fragment, dup. *VAB* VII p. 20 100-106.
K 19422 Uncertain.
K 19423 +K 2869+, dup. *CT* 17 26 86-87, Asaggig.
K 19424 Administrative/legal?
K 19425 Uncertain.
K 19426 Prayer?
K 19427 Administrative?
K 19428 Sennacherib royal inscription (prism fragment); third campaign?
K 19429 (+)Rm 930 (+)Rm II 289, An=Anum V 200-204.
K 19430 Neo-Assyrian administrative; list of personal names.
K 19431 +K 9022+, Ḫulbazizi 112-118.
K 19432 Diagnostic omens?
K 19433 Legal.
K 19434 Bab.
K 19435 Literary/religious?
K 19436 Uncertain.
K 19437 Uncertain.
K 19438 Uncertain.
K 19439 Uncertain.
K 19440 Uncertain.
K 19441 Neo-Assyrian administrative, textiles.
K 19442 Literary/religious?
K 19443 Omens, see K 19389, K 19479.
K 19444 (+)K 7027+, Tamītu.
K 19445 Uncertain.
K 19446 Literary/religious.
K 19447 Listing of geographical names.
K 19448 Neo-Assyrian royal inscription.
K 19449 +K 2016b, dup. *ZA* 16 160 31-36, Lamaštu incantation.
K 19450 Literary/religious.
K 19451 Royal dedication inscription.
K 19452 Uncertain.
K 19453 Uncertain.
K 19454 Laws of Hammurabi?
K 19455 Dup. *STT* 252 2-9 etc., incantation prayer (Reiner, *Poetry* pp. 94-100).
K 19456 +K 6556, Maqlû III 1-7.
K 19457 Coarse Bab.

K 19458 Literary/religious.
K 19459 Astrological omens.
K 19460 Uncertain.
K 19461 Bab. Medical?
K 19462 Omens.
K 19463 Omens?
K 19464 Ritual?
K 19465 Uncertain.
K 19466 Omens?
K 19467 Omens.
K 19468 Emesal litany.
K 19469 Magico-medical?
K 19470 Prayer.
K 19471 Uncertain.
K 19472 About fields.
K 19473 Neo-Assyrian administrative?
K 19474 Bilingual?
K 19475 +K 8996+, Akkadian incantation, Lamaštu II 8-18.
K 19476 Omens.
K 19477 Ritual.
K 19478 Neo-Assyrian legal.
K 19479 ^{mul}APIN II iv 4-7 or Enūma Anu Enlil LV? Cf. K 19389, K19443.
K 19480 Magico-medical or literary/religious?
K 19481 Omens?
K 19482 Ritual concerning images of sorcerers.
K 19483 Omens?
K 19484 Literary/religious/medical.
K 19485 Extispicy; reverse sideways to obverse.
K 19486 Literary/religious.
K 19487 Bilingual, Lugale 72-73?
K 19488 Yellow clay, large script.
K 19489 +K 9550 (*BL* 133), Sumerian litany.
K 19490 Literary/royal inscription?
K 19491 Literary/religious.
K 19492 "URUxGU".
K 19493 Days of the month listed.
K 19494 Omens?
K 19495 "Canonical" Temple list.
K 19496 Bab. Omens, ḪAL repeated.
K 19497 Omens?
K 19498 Omens.
K 19499 Eršemma.
K 19500 Uncertain.
K 19501 Letter?
K 19502 Aa 6 17-20 (*MSL* XIV 225).
K 19503 Uncertain.
K 19504 Ashurbanipal colophon.
K 19505 Medical.
K 19506 Bab. Medical
K 19507 Uncertain.
K 19508 Omens.
K 19509 Uncertain.
K 19510 Omens; "*ina* ḫi.gar" five times.
K 19511 Ashurbanipal colophon.
K 19512 Literary?
K 19513 Uncertain.
K 19514 Omens.
K 19515 Bilingual?
K 19516 Uncertain.
K 19517 Bab. Letter?
K 19518 Omens?
K 19519 Astrological omens.
K 19520 Neo-Assyrian letter.
K 19521 Listing of temples; Götteradressbuch?
K 19522 Bab. Literary/religious?
K 19523 Omens?
K 19524 Omens?
K 19525 Bilingual Eršaḫunga, Maul p. 374-375, pl. 61*.
K 19526 Colophon.
K 19527 Bilingual Eršaḫunga, Maul p. 325, pl. 61*.
K 19528 (+)K 8532+, king list, see K 16801.
K 19529 Ušburruda?
K 19530 +Rm II 454+, Etana (ed. J. V. Kinnier Wilson pls. 24-25*).
K 19531 Bab. Astrological omens.
K 19532 Dup. *CT* 16 19-20 59-68, Udugḫul XVI.

K 19533 Omens?
K 19534 +K 9876 (Pallis, *Akîtu* pls. 8-11), ritual for New Year in Babylon.
K 19535 Prayer.
K 19536 Uncertain.
K 19537 Uncertain.
K 19538 Literary/religious.
K 19539 Prayer, incipit ending "*mālik Igīgi*".
K 19540 Bab. Bilingual?
K 19541 Colophon.
K 19542 Omens?
K 19543 Literary/religious?
K 19544 Neo-Assyrian letter, to the king.
K 19545 Neo-Assyrian administrative.
K 19546 Ashurbanipal colophon.
K 19547 Lexical, professional titles.
K 19548 Bilingual.
K 19549 Gilgameš VIII 45-49 and vi 1-2.
K 19550 Uncertain.
K 19551 Fable of Spider?
K 19552 +K 4903+, bilingual litany, *CLAM* p. 689 e+116ff., cf. B. Alster, *BBVO* 6 20.
K 19553 Literary/religious.
K 19554 Bab.
K 19555 Omens? (First "*pirsu*").
K 19556 Bilingual Eršaḫunga, Maul p. 272, pl. 42*.
K 19557 Ritual involving images.
K 19558 Ashurbanipal colophon.
K 19559 Laws of Hammurabi §§58, 59, 66.
K 19560 Uncertain.
K 19561 Bab. Literary/religious.
K 19562 Literary/religious.
K 19563 Uncertain.
K 19564 Bab. Letter.
K 19565 Colophon?
K 19566 Omens.
K 19567 Literary/religious?
K 19568 Large script.
K 19569 Bilingual.
K 19570 Hymn.
K 19571 Lexical list, section on [*ūru/biṣṣūru*].
K 19572 "Šulpa[e]".
K 19573 Bilingual, Lugale 438-441.
K 19574 +K 13532, bilingual hymn/prayer to Ashur?
K 19575 Bilingual religious.
K 19576 Bilingual, beginning "im.dugu[d.gim] = *ki-ma as*-[*suk-ki*]".
K 19577 Šuilla to Ištar, dup. *STC* II pl. lxxv 8-14.
K 19578 Omens.
K 19579 Gattung I, dup. E. Ebeling, *ArOr* 21 377 12-18.
K 19580 Neo-Assyrian royal inscription.
K 19581 Ashurbanipal colophon.
K 19582 Bilingual religious.
K 19583 Uncertain ("*išpatu*").
K 19584 Bab.
K 19585 Religious?
K 19586 Uncertain.
K 19587 +K 4623+ (*OECT* VI pl. XIX), Maul p. 296, pl. 46*, bilingual Eršaḫunga.
K 19588 Neo-Assyrian letter to the king.
K 19589 Bab. Literary/religious?
K 19590 Sumerian incantation, dup. K 5036+, 5127, 9336+, 10111, 10809, 13419, Rm II 337, BM 121045+.
K 19591 Neo-Assyrian letter?
K 19592 Sumerian, religious.
K 19593 Bilingual religious?
K 19594 Incantation.
K 19595 Omens.
K 19596 Fable of the Ox?
K 19597 Bab. Colophon.
K 19598 Bilingual incantation, "Marduk-Ea type".
K 19599 Neo-Assyrian legal, conveyance.
K 19600 Dup. *CT* 16 1 23-27, Udugḫul III.

K 19601 Uncertain.
K 19602 Omens.
K 19603 Literary/religious.
K 19604 (+)K 3478 (*AnSt* 6 148), The Poor Man of Nippur 19-25.
K 19605 Uncertain.
K 19606 Bilingual Eršaḫunga, cf. Maul p. 94.
K 19607 +Rm 306+ (IV R^2, Add. p. 10 15-20), royal ritual.
K 19608 Lugale 1-2, ed. van Dijk pl. lxxvii*).
K 19609 +79-7-8, 93 (*AMT* 51 8), cf. K 307 (*BAM* VI 563), medical.
K 19610 Uncertain.
K 19611 Bab. Omens.
K 19612 Magic. Namburbi?
K 19613 Sumerian.
K 19614 +K 13867, Enūma eliš VI 117-123.
K 19615 Ashurbanipal colophon.
K 19616 Love lyrics, dup. *Unity and Diversity* p. 122 7-17.
K 19617 Uncertain.
K 19618 Love lyrics, dup. *Unity and Diversity* p. 114 K 7924 rev. iv.
K 19619 Bilingual.
K 19620 Literary/religious.
K 19621 Neo-Assyrian letter.
K 19622 Neo-Assyrian letter?
K 19623 Dup. *AOAT* I p. 6 §XIII, bilingual incantation.
K 19624 Bab. Bilingual?
K 19625 Uncertain.
K 19626 Uncertain.
K 19627 Bab. Letter.
K 19628 Medical.
K 19629 Hymn/prayer?
K 19630 Letter?
K 19631 Literary/religious?
K 19632 Sumerian religious?
K 19633 Sumerian, Eršaḫunga (Maul p. 348, pl. 55*).
K 19634 Uncertain.
K 19635 Sumerian litany.
K 19636 Bab. Literary?
K 19637 Magic, perhaps Namburbi?
K 19638 Sumerian litany, Ukkinta ešbar tilla, (+)K 3238+, dup. *CLAM* pp. 483-484, 60-65.
K 19639 Love lyrics, dup. *Unity and Diversity* pp. 108-110 8-22.
K 19640 Uncertain.
K 19641 Extispicy or medical.
K 19642 Magical. Perhaps Ušburruda.
K 19643 Bilingual religious.
K 19644 Religious.
K 19645 Uncertain.
K 19646 Dup. *CT* 16 5 190-195, Udugḫul III.
K 19647 Ritual?
K 19648 List?
K 19649 Library text.
K 19650 Literary/religious.
K 19651 Royal inscription of Ashurbanipal, Egyptian campaign; from tablet.
K 19652 Library text.
K 19653 Religious.
K 19654 Omens.
K 19655 Bulla with Neo-Assyrian royal (stamp) seal type.
K 19656 Hymn.
K 19657 Hymn, to Ningirsu(?).
K 19658 Prayer or ritual.
K 19659 Colophon?
K 19660 Amulet stones.
K 19661 Fragment of bulla with Neo-Assyrian royal (stamp) seal type.
K 19662 Bab.
K 19663 Marble fragment with two signs.
K 19664 Literary/religious.
K 19665 Fragment of bulla with stamp seal impression showing god in crescent boat.
K 19666 Bab. Omens?
K 19667 Uncertain.
K 19668 Uncertain.

K 19669 “*šerru*”.
K 19670 Prism fragment, Ashurbanipal royal inscription, dup. *VAB* VII 42 126-130.
K 19671 Ištar hymn.
K 19672 Omens.
K 19673 Neo-Assyrian letter, *SAA* I 27*.
K 19674 Piece of envelope.
K 19675 Incantations, related to *AfO* 23 42f. 20ff.
K 19676 Neo-Assyrian letter?
K 19677 Uncertain.
K 19678 Uncertain.
K 19679 Uncertain.
K 19680 Library text.
K 19681 +DT 162. Ashurbanipal prism fragment, dup. *VAB* VII p. 90 116-120.
K 19682 Literary/religious.
K 19683 Neo-Assyrian letter?
K 19684 Uncertain.
K 19685 Omens, rev. dup. *DA* p. 16 14-16.
K 19686 Uncertain.
K 19687 End of library text with colophon?
K 19688 Uncertain.
K 19689 “*ḫanšu*”.
K 19690 Bulla with incomplete Neo-Assyrian royal (stamp) seal type.
K 19691 Uncertain.
K 19692 Litany?
K 19693 Late Babylonian legal or administrative, cf. K 18772.
K 19694 Uncertain.
K 19695 +K 3238. Bilingual litany, Ukkinta ešbar tilla, *CLAM* p. 483 56-57.
K 19696 Uncertain.
K 19697 Omens.
K 19698 Ashurbanipal colophon.
K 19699 Bilingual?
K 19700 Bab. Omens?
K 19701 Library text.
K 19702 Ritual or omens?
K 19703 Literary or prayer?
K 19704 Incantations.
K 19705 Incantations.
K 19706 +K 19721. Sumerian litany, dup. *SBH* p. 99 71ff. See Cohen, *Eršemma* p. 9 34.
K 19707 Prayer to Šamaš, *UFBG* p. 419 78.
K 19708 Omens?
K 19709 List of Enlil’s ancestors, from zi ... pà context?
K 19710 Bab. Omens.
K 19711 Bab. Marduk prayer, *UFBG* p. 397 15?
K 19712 Bilingual?
K 19713 Šuilla prayer to Tašmētum, *UFBG* p. 423, Tašmētu 1.
K 19714 Incantation.
K 19715 Bilingual?
K 19716 Omens.
K 19717 Uncertain.
K 19718 Library text.
K 19719 Bilingual litany.
K 19720 Omens?
K 19721 +K 19706 (which see).
K 19722 Uncertain.
K 19723 Uncertain.
K 19724 List?
K 19725 Literary/religious?
K 19726 Bilingual exorcistic.
K 19727 Laws of Hammurabi?
K 19728 Omens?
K 19729 Omens?
K 19730 Medical.
K 19731 Medical.
K 19732 Bab. Sumerian?
K 19733 Colophon(?) naming Sennacherib.
K 19734 Ashurbanipal colophon.
K 19735 Lexical.
K 19736 Uncertain.
K 19737 Lexical.
K 19738 Omens?

K 19739 Omens?
K 19740 (+)Rm 287, dup. *STT* 71, BM 76762 (*RA* 53 134ff.), prayer to Nabû.
K 19741 Literary/religious?
K 19742 Uncertain.
K 19743 Literary/religious?
K 19744 Medical.
K 19745 Bilingual, cf. *CT* 17 41, K 2873 9-10.
K 19746 Uncertain, perhaps colophon?
K 19747 Bab. Omens?
K 19748 Coarse script, Neo-Assyrian letter.
K 19749 Sumerian litany, cf. Sm 355 (*BL* 33).
K 19750 Colophon?
K 19751 Literary. Erra myth?
K 19752 Bilingual incantation, cf. *ZA* 45 26 4-10 and K 20274.
K 19753 Colophon, "11th *pirsu*".
K 19754 Liver omens?
K 19755 Commentary on Šumma izbu V 62, 84-93.
K 19756 Bilingual?
K 19757 +K 10182. Catalogue of library texts, (M. Lebeau and P. Talon, eds., *Reflets des deux fleuves* (Akkadica Supplementum VI; Leuven, 1989). 95, 98*).
K 19758 Tintir = Bābilu IV 7-11.
K 19759 Uncertain.
K 19760 Ashurbanipal colophon.
K 19761 Library text.
K 19762 +K 4995, see K 17250.
K 19763 Omens.
K 19764 Coarse script, library text.
K 19765 Liver omens.
K 19766 Dup. K 2574+ (*BAM* V 482 ii 27-33, see p. xxvi), medical. (+)K 6066+?
K 19767 Uncertain.
K 19768 Ikrib.
K 19769 Bab. Diagnostic omens.
K 19770 Uncertain.
K 19771 Library text.
K 19772 Royal inscription?
K 19773 Omens.
K 19774 Medical, perhaps dúr.gig.
K 19775 Colophon.
K 19776 Bab. Prayer.
K 19777 Literary/religious.
K 19778 Amulet stones?
K 19779 Coarse script, Neo-Assyrian letter.
K 19780 Lugale 262-264, ed. van Dijk pl. lxxvii*.
K 19781 Ritual.
K 19782 Dup. *CLAM* pp. 256f. 52-59, Sumerian litany, cf. K 17251+.
K 19783 Omens.
K 19784 Uncertain.
K 19785 +K 11904, bilingual Eršaḫunga, Maul p. 345, pl. 55*.
K 19786 Bab. Bilingual Eršaḫunga, Maul p. 375, pl. 62*.
K 19787 Neo-Assyrian letter.
K 19788 Library text.
K 19789 +K 9906, bilingual hymn to Nanay, *JNES* 33 227-228 40-43, (+)K 3933, 11778.
K 19790 Large, coarse script. Administrative?
K 19791 Bab. Omens.
K 19792 Omens or ritual?
K 19793 Uncertain.
K 19794 Literary/religious.
K 19795 Bilingual prayer, cf. IV R^2 19 no. 3 39-40.
K 19796 +K 5087+, dup. *CT* 17 39-40 73-79, bilingual incantation. See K 17627.
K 19797 Šurpu II 52-60, (+)K 5495, 6432, 6432a, 14217.
K 19798 Uncertain.
K 19799 Omens.
K 19800 Religious text from the reforms of Sennacherib?

K 19801 Bab. Omens.
K 19802 "*izbi alpi*".
K 19803 Literary/religious.
K 19804 Omens?
K 19805 Omens, medical?
K 19806 Incantation?
K 19807 Library text.
K 19808 Bab. Library text.
K 19809 Dup. *CT* 16 10 40-47; Udugḫul IV. See K 18329.
K 19810 Omens.
K 19811 Ritual.
K 19812 Omens.
K 19813 Ritual?
K 19814 Library text.
K 19815 Magic? Medical?
K 19816 Bab. Emesal bilingual.
K 19817 Medical.
K 19818 Uncertain.
K 19819 Omens.
K 19820 Royal dedication inscription.
K 19821 Magic?
K 19822 Literary/religious.
K 19823 Omens.
K 19824 Religious or legal?
K 19825 God list.
K 19826 Bilingual, Inanna of Uruk lament.
K 19827 Bab. Dup. *SBH* p. 115 30-35 (*CLAM* pp. 639f. 33-35), bilingual litany. Cf. K 17455.
K 19828 Religious/literary.
K 19829 Omens.
K 19830 Bilingual Eršaḫunga, Maul p. 106, pl. 10*.
K 19831 Medical, dup. *BAM* VI 522 3-8.
K 19832 Each line begins: "máš.sag".
K 19833 Uncertain.
K 19834 Uncertain.
K 19835 Literary/religious.
K 19836 Sumerian text, naming "d]úb-li-[áš"?
K 19837 Prayers?
K 19838 Bab. Ritual.
K 19839 Uncertain.
K 19840 Uncertain.
K 19841 Library text.
K 19842 Bab. Omens.
K 19843 Omens.
K 19844 Omens?
K 19845 Omens?
K 19846 Library text.
K 19847 Coarse Bab.
K 19848 Middle Assyrian script. Sumerian.
K 19849 Omens.
K 19850 Bilingual.
K 19851 Bilingual Eršaḫunga, Maul p. 181-182*.
K 19852 Uncertain.
K 19853 Omens?
K 19854 (+)K 5040+ (*BL* 179), Sumerian litany.
K 19855 Bab. Astrological omens?
K 19856 Omens.
K 19857 Ritual.
K 19858 Religious/literary.
K 19859 Uncertain.
K 19860 Large script.
K 19861 Royal inscription of Sennacherib?
K 19862 Omens?
K 19863 Literary/religious?
K 19864 +K 6070. Bab. Prayers.
K 19865 Uncertain.
K 19866 Omens?
K 19867 Uncertain.
K 19868 Literary/religious?
K 19869 Omens.
K 19870 Incantations?
K 19871 Uncertain.
K 19872 Liver omens.
K 19873 Uncertain.
K 19874 Uncertain.
K 19875 Omens?
K 19876 Uncertain.
K 19877 Omens.
K 19878 Uncertain.

K 19879 Laws of Hammurabi §166.
K 19880 Bab. Literary/religious?
K 19881 Lexical, synonym list?
K 19882 Bilingual, incantations or wisdom?
K 19883 Religious, bilingual?
K 19884 Uncertain.
K 19885 Amuletic stones?
K 19886 Hymn/prayer?
K 19887 Omens.
K 19888 Uncertain.
K 19889 Letter?
K 19890 Uncertain.
K 19891 Letter?
K 19892 Library text.
K 19893 Colophon.
K 19894 Uncertain.
K 19895 Uncertain.
K 19896 Uncertain.
K 19897 Library text.
K 19898 Bilingual.
K 19899 Uncertain.
K 19900 Ušburruda?
K 19901 Bilingual.
K 19902 Uncertain.
K 19903 Uncertain.
K 19904 Omens/ritual.
K 19905 Uncertain.
K 19906 Diagnostic omens?
K 19907 Medical.
K 19908 Literary/religious, "*namtar, murṣu*".
K 19909 Uncertain.
K 19910 Uncertain.
K 19911 Religious?
K 19912 Uncertain.
K 19913 Uncertain.
K 19914 Uncertain.
K 19915 Religious/literary.
K 19916 Bilingual?
K 19917 +K 2728+, Maqlû III 186-191.
K 19918 Lexical or litany?
K 19919 Uncertain.
K 19920 Incantation.
K 19921 Omens?
K 19922 Uncertain.
K 19923 Uncertain.
K 19924 Uncertain.
K 19925 Omens?
K 19926 Bilingual incantation.
K 19927 Bilingual?
K 19928 Tamītu?
K 19929 Omens.
K 19930 Neo-Assyrian letter or administrative.
K 19931 Neo-Assyrian letter.
K 19932 Hymn to goddess.
K 19933 Ritual.
K 19934 Bab. Omens?
K 19935 Bab. Astrological.
K 19936 Omens?
K 19937 Bilingual.
K 19938 Neo-Assyrian letter?
K 19939 Colophon.
K 19940 Lexical.
K 19941 Bab.
K 19942 Sumerian.
K 19943 (+)K 5120, Udugḫul XV 85-87, see *CT* 16 46 163-167.
K 19944 Omens?
K 19945 Bilingual.
K 19946 Bilingual, Emesal litany.
K 19947 Meteorological omens.
K 19948 Bab. Prayer?
K 19949 Lexical?
K 19950 "K Mound". Uncertain.
K 19951 Literary/religious?
K 19952 Prayer?
K 19953 Love lyrics, (+)K 4247+ (*Unity and Diversity* pp. 129-130)?
K 19954 Literary/religious.
K 19955 Uncertain.
K 19956 Uncertain.
K 19957 +Rm II 475 +79-7-8, 64, Bīt mēseri.
K 19958 Literary/religious.
K 19959 Library text.
K 19960 Omens?

K 19961 Bilingual?
K 19962 "SW IV 20". Colophon of tablet with [Xx]60+12 lines.
K 19963 Ashurbanipal colophon.
K 19964 Literary/religious.
K 19965 Neo-Assyrian letter.
K 19966 Bab. Letter.
K 19967 Uncertain.
K 19968 Uncertain.
K 19969 Bab. Letter, cf. K 19966?
K 19970 Omens.
K 19971 Neo-Assyrian letter?
K 19972 Uncertain.
K 19973 Neo-Assyrian letter.
K 19974 Bab. Letter.
K 19975 Bab. Letter.
K 19976 Uncertain.
K 19977 Medical?
K 19978 Bab. Letter.
K 19979 Neo-Assyrian letter.
K 19980 Bab. Letter?
K 19981 Omens.
K 19982 Uncertain.
K 19983 Neo-Assyrian letter.
K 19984 Omens?
K 19985 Ritual.
K 19986 Neo-Assyrian letter.
K 19987 Royal inscription.
K 19988 Library text.
K 19989 Bab. Letter.
K 19990 Neo-Assyrian letter.
K 19991 Uncertain.
K 19992 Neo-Assyrian letter.
K 19993 Omens?
K 19994 Neo-Assyrian letter, *SAA* I no. 60, p. 255*.
K 19995 Bilingual incantation.
K 19996 Uncertain.
K 19997 Bab. Letter.
K 19998 Bab. Letter.
K 19999 Neo-Assyrian letter.
K 20000 Neo-Assyrian letter.
K 20001 Omens.
K 20002 Uncertain.
K 20003 Uncertain.
K 20004 Bab. Administrative.
K 20005 Omens.
K 20006 Uncertain.
K 20007 Uncertain.
K 20008 Uncertain.
K 20009 Neo-Assyrian letter.
K 20010 Uncertain.
K 20011 Bilingual. Cf. K 18899.
K 20012 Uncertain.
K 20013 (+)K 2589, Gilgameš VII iv.
K 20014 Administrative?
K 20015 Middle Assyrian script, +K 1621a vi 54-62 (*AKA* 84f.), royal inscription of Tiglath-pileser I.
K 20016 Omens?
K 20017 Emesal Eršaḫunga, Maul p. 69, pl. 5*.
K 20018 Omens.
K 20019 Middle Assyrian script, +K 1621a vi 50-55 (*AKA* 83f.), royal inscription of Tiglath-pileser I.
K 20020 Prayer?
K 20021 Omens.
K 20022 Omens.
K 20023 Omens (months in succession).
K 20024 Omens?
K 20025 Library text?
K 20026 Bilingual.
K 20027 Uncertain.
K 20028 Omens?
K 20029 Omens.
K 20030 Literary/incantation?
K 20031 Letter?
K 20032 Uncertain.
K 20033 Bilingual.
K 20034 Bab.
K 20035 Bab. Religious?
K 20036 Lexical?
K 20037 Uncertain.
K 20038 Literary/religious?
K 20039 Uncertain.

K 20040 Omens.
K 20041 Omens.
K 20042 "K 2". Prayer?
K 20043 Maqlû(-type) incantation.
K 20044 Lexical.
K 20045 Medical.
K 20046 Magic?
K 20047 Omens.
K 20048 Bab. Letter?
K 20049 Omens.
K 20050 Bab. Letter?
K 20051 Bulla with seal impression of standing god in crescent boat.
K 20052 Omens.
K 20053 Middle Assyrian script, royal inscription of Tiglath-pileser I, dup. *AKA* p. 72 42ff.
K 20054 Ritual.
K 20055 Hymn?
K 20056 Omens.
K 20057 Uncertain.
K 20058 Uncertain.
K 20059 Liver omens.
K 20060 Omens (Šumma ālu?).
K 20061 Sumerian or bilingual?
K 20062 Coarse Bab.
K 20063 Astrological omens?
K 20064 Uncertain.
K 20065 Omens.
K 20066 Bab.
K 20067 Uncertain.
K 20068 Uncertain.
K 20069 Bab. Letter?
K 20070 Bilingual? Cf. K 20074.
K 20071 Literary/religious.
K 20072 Bab.
K 20073 Incantation and ritual.
K 20074 Sumerian? Cf. K 20070.
K 20075 Library text.
K 20076 Astrology?
K 20077 Hymn?
K 20078 Medical?
K 20079 Literary/religious.
K 20080 Library text.
K 20081 Bab. Astrological omens.
K 20082 Medical.
K 20083 Listing of years and intercalary months.
K 20084 +K 11233+. Malku=šarru IV.
K 20085 Star names.
K 20086 Bab. Literary/religious.
K 20087 Bab. About arable farming.
K 20088 Omens.
K 20089 Dup. *MVAG* 40/2 pp. 78-80 74-82, (+)K 2335+, physiognomic omens.
K 20090 Omens?
K 20091 Emesal litany.
K 20092 Historical epic?
K 20093 Uncertain.
K 20094 Bilingual Eršaḫunga, Maul p. 376 pl. 62*.
K 20095 Royal inscription?
K 20096 Administrative.
K 20097 Library text.
K 20098 +K 4615+17479; see the latter.
K 20099 Omens.
K 20100 Omens.
K 20101 Bilingual.
K 20102 Omens?
K 20103 Omens?
K 20104 Magico-medical.
K 20105 Bab. Literary/religious.
K 20106 Magico-medical?
K 20107 Library text.
K 20108 Medical.
K 20109 Uncertain.
K 20110 Uncertain.
K 20111 Omens.
K 20112 Literary?
K 20113 Literary/religious.
K 20114 Omens.
K 20115 Uncertain.
K 20116 Library text.
K 20117 Uncertain.
K 20118 Uncertain.
K 20119 God list?

K 20120 +K 5135, dup. *JCS* 21 6-7 47-53, Bīt rimki, House III.
K 20121 Neo-Assyrian text, letter?
K 20122 Request for blessings.
K 20123 Mentions watches of the night.
K 20124 Omens concerning the tongue.
K 20125 Medical.
K 20126 Medical, cf. K 20129?
K 20127 Omens.
K 20128 Medical,
K 20129 Medical, cf. K 20126?
K 20130 Omens.
K 20131 Medical or magic.
K 20132 Medical.
K 20133 Literary/religious.
K 20134 Concerns the *egubbû*.
K 20135 Bab. Incantation/medical?
K 20136 Medical.
K 20137 Bab. Medical.
K 20138 Medical.
K 20139 Incantation and rituals.
K 20140 Medical.
K 20141 +K 203+ (Oppenheim, *Glass* p. 37 1´-3´), glass making.
K 20142 Ritual?
K 20143 Medical.
K 20144 Uncertain.
K 20145 Bab. Magic?
K 20146 Bilingual?
K 20147 Literary/religious?
K 20148 Historical epic.
K 20149 Bilingual.
K 20150 Synonym list or commentary?
K 20151 +Sm 1564, Marduk's Ordeal (*NABU* 1987/68; *SAA* III 35-42*).
K 20152 Literary/religious.
K 20153 Exorcistic?
K 20154 Epic?
K 20155 +K 163+, Marduk prayer (*Iraq* 31 85 38-46), cf. K 17478.
K 20156 Literary/religious.
K 20157 Šumma ālu?
K 20158 Scholarly text.
K 20159 Incantations?
K 20160 Bilingual litany.
K 20161 Library text.
K 20162 Religious.
K 20163 Incantation.
K 20164 Epic?
K 20165 Bilingual exorcism?
K 20166 Incantation.
K 20167 Coarse Bab.
K 20168 Medical? Cf. K 4082+.
K 20169 Uncertain.
K 20170 Uncertain.
K 20171 Uncertain.
K 20172 Literary.
K 20173 Uncertain.
K 20174 Uncertain.
K 20175 Bab.
K 20176 Uncertain.
K 20177 Uncertain,
K 20178 Hymn or Neo-Assyrian royal inscription.
K 20179 (+)K 2497+ (*AMT* 92 4) obv. 1, medical.
K 20180 Uncertain.
K 20181 Liver omens.
K 20182 Literary/religious.
K 20183 Erased.
K 20184 Uncertain.
K 20185 Uncertain.
K 20186 Uncertain.
K 20187 Uncertain.
K 20188 Uncertain.
K 20189 Uncertain.
K 20190 Late Babylonian legal or administrative. See K 18772.
K 20191 +K 4943+ (*CT* 16 12 i 1-5), Udugḫul V.
K 20192 Uncertain.
K 20193 Uncertain.
K 20194 Uncertain.
K 20195 Bab. Medical.
K 20196 Ritual?
K 20197 Bilingual?
K 20198 Library text.

K 20199 Uncertain.
K 20200 Literary?
K 20201 Uncertain.
K 20202 Omens.
K 20203 Literary.
K 20204 Uncertain.
K 20205 Uncertain.
K 20206 Bab.
K 20207 Coarse script.
K 20208 Coarse script. Astrology.
K 20209 Coarse script. Bab.?
K 20210 Coarse script.
K 20211 Coarse script. About omens?
K 20212 Coarse script.
K 20213 +K 20297. Coarse script. Omens?
K 20214 Coarse Bab.
K 20215 Bab.
K 20216 Coarse script. Bab.?
K 20217 Large, coarse script.
K 20218 Coarse script. Bab.?
K 20219 Coarse Bab.
K 20220 Neo-Assyrian administrative.
K 20221 Coarse Bab.
K 20222 Coarse script.
K 20223 Uncertain.
K 20224 Uncertain.
K 20225 Coarse script.
K 20226 Uncertain.
K 20227 Coarse Bab.
K 20228 Large, coarse script. Religious?
K 20229 Coarse Bab.
K 20230 Coarse script.
K 20231 Coarse script.
K 20232 Coarse Bab.
K 20233 Medical?
K 20234 Astrological omens?
K 20235 Coarse script.
K 20236 Coarse script.
K 20237 Neo-Assyrian administrative.
K 20238 +K 4891+, bilingual Eršaḫunga, Maul pp. 359-360, pl. 57*.
K 20239 Large, coarse script.
K 20240 Administrative?
K 20241 Royal inscription of Esarhaddon or Ashurbanipal?
K 20242 Middle Assyrian script. Royal inscription of Tiglath-pileser I, dup. *AKA* p. 36 76-82.
K 20243 Omens?
K 20244 Omens.
K 20245 Library text.
K 20246 Omens.
K 20247 Omens.
K 20248 Omens?
K 20249 Exorcisms.
K 20250 Uncertain.
K 20251 Omens.
K 20252 Uncertain.
K 20253 Ritual or medical?
K 20254 Bab. Medical, gynaecology. Cf. *BAM* 237, 240, 241.
K 20255 Library text.
K 20256 Omens.
K 20257 Library text.
K 20258 Bab. Administrative.
K 20259 Uncertain.
K 20260 Omens?
K 20261 Uncertain.
K 20262 Bab. Omens?
K 20263 Omens.
K 20264 Myth or epic.
K 20265 Bilingual Emesal litany, see J. A. Black, *BiOr* 44 40 B6.
K 20266 Literary?
K 20267 Medical?
K 20268 Lexical/commentary?
K 20269 Perhaps (+)K 5087+ (*CT* 17 40), bilingual incantation. See K 17627.
K 20270 Ritual.
K 20271 Religious?
K 20272 Coarse Bab.
K 20273 +K 2510 (*AMT* 30 6), medical.
K 20274 Bab. Bilingual incantation, dup. *ZA* 45 26 3-4 and K 19752.
K 20275 +K 20295 (+?)K 315, "Eršemma" repeated.

K 20276 Library text.
K 20277 Uncertain.
K 20278 Incantations and rituals.
K 20279 Bab.
K 20280 +K 8463+, Theodicy 2-12.
K 20281 +K 2368+, Laessøe, *Bīt rimki* pp. 39-40 41-55, pl. 2.
K 20282 Uncertain.
K 20283 Incantation?
K 20284 +K 9594 (*ZA* 4 249), cf. VAT 9427. Astrology.
K 20285 Prayer or Neo-Assyrian royal inscription.
K 20286 Omens.
K 20287 Uncertain.
K 20288 Literary/religious.
K 20289 Dup. *ASKT* p. 124 18-22, see K 17250.
K 20290 Hymn?
K 20291 Uncertain.
K 20292 Neo-Assyrian letter.
K 20293 Uncertain.
K 20294 Ritual or medical?
K 20295 +K 20275, which see.
K 20296 Library text.
K 20297 +K 20213, which see.
K 20298 Omens.
K 20299 Bab. Omens.
K 20300 Uncertain.
K 20301 Liver omens.
K 20302 Omens.
K 20303 Bab. Liver omens.
K 20304 Library text.
K 20305 Omens.
K 20306 Ritual?
K 20307 Ritual.
K 20308 Omens.
K 20309 Omens.
K 20310 Liver omens.
K 20311 Omens.
K 20312 Omens.
K 20313 Bab. Ritual or omens?
K 20314 Omens?
K 20315 Uncertain.
K 20316 Omens.
K 20317 Medical?
K 20318 Liver omens.
K 20319 Library text.
K 20320 Neo-Assyrian literary?
K 20321 Omens.
K 20322 Omens?
K 20323 Bilingual?
K 20324 Neo-Assyrian administrative.
K 20325 Bilingual.
K 20326 Library text.
K 20327 Medical?
K 20328 Omens.
K 20329 Bab. Administrative, about horses.
K 20330 Medical.
K 20331 Library text?
K 20332 Bab. Omens.
K 20333 Uncertain.
K 20334 Omens?
K 20335 Omens?
K 20336 Uncertain.
K 20337 Library text.
K 20338 Library text.
K 20339 Omens.
K 20340 Ritual for quietening a baby, Farber, *Schlaf, Kindschen, Schlaf!* p. 130, pl. 15*.
K 20341 Neo-Assyrian administrative.
K 20342 Omens (Šumma ālu?).
K 20343 Library text.
K 20344 Omens?
K 20345 Omens?
K 20346 Omens.
K 20347 Omens.
K 20348 Neo-Assyrian administrative (grant/census).
K 20349 Omens.
K 20350 Omens?
K 20351 Omens.
K 20352 Omens?
K 20353 +K 1753+ (*ADD* 465+), Neo-Assyrian administrative.
K 20354 Uncertain.

K 20355 Medical?
K 20356 Bab. Sumerian?
K 20357 Library text.
K 20358 +K 8427, bilingual Eršaḫunga, Maul p. 382, pl. 69*.
K 20359 Bilingual.
K 20360 +K 2257+, Udugḫul IV (*CT* 16 10 iv 47-53). Cf. K 18329.
K 20361 Bilingual.
K 20362 Exorcistic.
K 20363 End of bilingual exorcistic incantation.
K 20364 Library text.
K 20365 Sumerian.
K 20366 Ritual.
K 20367 Bilingual prayer.
K 20368 Sumerian.
K 20369 Sumerian?
K 20370 Uncertain.
K 20371 Sumerian or bilingual.
K 20372 Sumerian.
K 20373 Library text.
K 20374 Uncertain.
K 20375 +K 5007+, see K 18643.
K 20376 Library text.
K 20377 Bilingual or lexical.
K 20378 Bilingual.
K 20379 +K 9373 (*BL* 42), Emesal litany.
K 20380 Omens?
K 20381 Bilingual?
K 20382 Bilingual incantation. Udugḫul III?
K 20383 +K 4900+ (*CT* 17 39-40 74-84), bilingual incantation, see K 17627.
K 20384 +K 3586+ (*CT* 17 35 69-76), bilingual incantation. Cf. K 17151.
K 20385 Bilingual.
K 20386 Library text.
K 20387 Bilingual.
K 20388 Library text.
K 20389 Omens?
K 20390 Bilingual?
K 20391 Library text.
K 20392 Uncertain.
K 20393 Uncertain.
K 20394 Bab. Magic?
K 20395 (+)K 20410, liver omens.
K 20396 Lexical?
K 20397 Middle Assyrian script.
K 20398 Library text.
K 20399 Uncertain.
K 20400 Library text.
K 20401 Sumerian?
K 20402 Uncertain.
K 20403 Uncertain.
K 20404 Library text.
K 20405 Bab. Literary/religious.
K 20406 Uncertain.
K 20407 Neo-Assyrian letter?
K 20408 Bab.
K 20409 Uncertain.
K 20410 (+)K 20395, liver omens.
K 20411 Litany.
K 20412 Uncertain.
K 20413 Uncertain.
K 20414 +K 8787+, Neo-Assyrian administrative. See K 18983.
K 20415 Uncertain.
K 20416 Uncertain.
K 20417 Coarse Bab.
K 20418 Uncertain.
K 20419 Uncertain.
K 20420 Traces.
K 20421 Neo-Assyrian letter?
K 20422 Uncertain.
K 20423 Traces.
K 20424 Uncertain.
K 20425 Uncertain.
K 20426 Unusual Neo-Assyrian script.
K 20427 Neo-Assyrian royal dedication inscription?
K 20428 Uncertain.
K 20429 Bab. Library text.
K 20430 Bab. Star names.
K 20431 Uncertain.
K 20432 Rulings.

K 20433 Uncertain.
K 20434 Library text.
K 20435 Omens.
K 20436 Omens?
K 20437 Traces.
K 20438 Uncertain.
K 20439 Traces.
K 20440 Literary/religious?
K 20441 Traces.
K 20442 Prayer?
K 20443 Uncertain.
K 20444 Medical.
K 20445 Uncertain.
K 20446 Uncertain.
K 20447 Sumerian incantation.
K 20448 Bab. Religious?
K 20449 Traces.
K 20450 Coarse script.
K 20451 Uncertain.
K 20452 Uncertain.
K 20453 Traces of library text and colophon.
K 20454 Ashurbanipal colophon related to Hunger, *AOAT* 2 no. 321.
K 20455 Colophon of Ashurbanipal to tablet of Šumma ālu.
K 20456 Traces of library text and colophon.
K 20457 Ashurbanipal colophon.
K 20458 Ashurbanipal colophon.
K 20459 Colophon.
K 20460 Ashurbanipal colophon.
K 20461 Traces of library text and colophon.
K 20462 Bilingual text and colophon.
K 20463 Colophon.
K 20464 Library text and colophon.
K 20465 Colophon to tablet of Šumma ālu.
K 20466 Ashurbanipal colophon.
K 20467 End of library text, Ashurbanipal colophon.
K 20468 Uncertain.
K 20469 Colophon, "tablet of Bēl-n[a- ...".
K 20470 End of library text, colophon.
K 20471 Colophon.
K 20472 +K 20505+20521 (+)K 11802. See K 17250.
K 20473 Ashurbanipal colophon. Cf. K 20454.
K 20474 Colophon? Very large script.
K 20475 Colophon.
K 20476 Uncertain.
K 20477 Ashurbanipal colophon.
K 20478 Ashurbanipal colophon.
K 20479 Ashurbanipal colophon.
K 20480 Ashurbanipal colophon.
K 20481 Ashurbanipal colophon.
K 20482 Ashurbanipal colophon.
K 20483 Ashurbanipal colophon.
K 20484 Colophon.
K 20485 Colophon.
K 20486 Commentary on Enūma Anu Enlil and colophon.
K 20487 Colophon.
K 20488 Colophon?
K 20489 End of library text, colophon.
K 20490 Prayer?
K 20491 Colophon.
K 20492 End of text, Ashurbanipal colophon.
K 20493 Nabû-zuqup-kēna colophon.
K 20494 Colophon.
K 20495 Colophon, "Written by Ashur-nādin-.[...]".
K 20496 Colophon.
K 20497 Library text with Nabû-zuqup-kēna colophon.
K 20498 Colophon.
K 20499 Traces of colophon.
K 20500 Ashurbanipal colophon.
K 20501 Ashurbanipal colophon.
K 20502 Colophon.
K 20503 Colophon.
K 20504 Colophon.
K 20505 +K 20472, which see.

K 20506 Colophon.
K 20507 Colophon.
K 20508 Colophon to medical text (*erītu*).
K 20509 Sumerian litany.
K 20510 Colophon?
K 20511 Colophon.
K 20512 Colophon.
K 20513 Ashurbanipal colophon.
K 20514 Colophon.
K 20515 Ashurbanipal colophon.
K 20516 Colophon.
K 20517 +K 14428 (*RA* 17 172), Malku=šarru IV.
K 20518 Medical?
K 20519 Colophon.
K 20520 Uncertain.
K 20521 +K 20472, which see.
K 20522 Colophon.
K 20523 End of library text and colophon.
K 20524 Colophon.
K 20525 Colophon.
K 20526 Ashurbanipal colophon.
K 20527 Colophon.
K 20528 +K 5449a+, Nabnītu VI i 8-15, ii 3-10 (*MSL* XVI 100-101).
K 20529 +Rm 483 (*CT* 25 47), god list.
K 20530 +K 7164 (*JNES* 15 138-9), Lipšur litany, dup. *JCS* 1 330-331 and ND 4385+4405/77.
K 20531 Dup. *BAM* 556 ii 67-iii, medical.
K 20532 Tamītu.
K 20533 Sumerian incantation. Mīs pî V?
K 20534 +K 15265+20535+20540+, Neo-Assyrian legal, *NALK* no. 335.
K 20535 See K 20534.
K 20536 +Rm 53 (*ADD* 338), Neo-Assyrian administrative.
K 20537 "Canonical" Temple list.
K 20538 Lugale 526-529, ed. van Dijk pl. lxxxvii*.
K 20539 "Rm". Neo-Assyrian legal document.
K 20540 See K 20534.
K 20541 "Rm". Neo-Assyrian legal document.
K 20542 "Rm". Neo-Assyrian administrative?
K 20543 Neo-Assyrian legal/administrative.
K 20544 Neo-Assyrian legal.
K 20545 Library text.
K 20546 "Rm". (+)K 4349+, Middle Assyrian script. God list, cf. K 20549.
K 20547 Sumerian incantations.
K 20548 Library text.
K 20549 "Rm". (+)K 4349+, Middle Assyrian script. God list, cf. K. 20546.
K 20550 Library text.
K 20551 Prayer.
K 20552 Bab.
K 20553 Uncertain.
K 20554 +K 4994+, bilingual incantation, dup. Farber, *Ištar und Dumuzi* p. 61 62-67.
K 20555 +Sm 554+, bilingual incantation, Reiner, *Šurpu* p. 52 8-16.
K 20556 "Rm". Neo-Assyrian letter.
K 20557 "Rm". Neo-Assyrian letter.
K 20558 "Rm". Neo-Assyrian legal document.
K 20559 "Rm". Library text?
K 20560 "Rm". Uncertain.
K 20561 "Rm". Uncertain.
K 20562 "Rm". Uncertain.
K 20563 "Rm". Uncertain.
K 20564 "Rm". Uncertain.
K 20565 Neo-Assyrian letter.
K 20566 "Rm". Bab. Letter.
K 20567 "Rm". Bab. Letter?
K 20568 "Rm". Bab. Letter.
K 20569 "Rm". Bab.
K 20570 "Rm". Bab. Letter.
K 20571 +Rm 86+ (*CT* 20 6), liver omens.

K 20572 "81-2-4". +81-2-4, 267+ (*CT* 14 36), plant list.
K 20573 Piece of bulla with stamp seal impressions, including god standing in crescent.
K 20574 Piece of bulla with stamp seal impression.
K 20575 Piece of bulla with stamp seal impression.
K 20576 Piece of bulla with stamp seal impressions.
K 20577 Piece of bulla with stamp seal impression.
K 20578 Piece of bulla with stamp seal impressions.
K 20579 Piece of bulla with stamp seal impressions.
K 20580 Piece of bulla with stamp seal impression.
K 20580 Piece of bulla with stamp seal impression.
K 20581 Piece of bulla with stamp seal impressions.
K 20582 Piece of bulla with stamp seal impression.
K 20583 Uncertain.
K 20584 Marks on vessel.
K 20585 Uncertain.
K 20586 Literary?
K 20587 Fragment of *sikkatu*.
K 20588 "79-7-8". Uncertain.
K 20589 Literary/religious?
K 20590 Uncertain.
K 20591 Library text.
K 20592 Uncertain.
K 20593 Uncertain.
K 20594 Uncertain.
K 20595 God list or catalogue of Sumerian texts.
K 20596 Bab. Astrology?
K 20597 "82-3-23". Uncertain.
K 20598 Uncertain.
K 20599 Sennacherib prism, cf. 89-4-26, 170 and BM 121030.
K 20600 Šumma ālu LX, dup. K 2922+ obv. 7-15 (*CT* 39 13).
K 20601 Uncertain.
K 20602 Literary/religious.
K 20603 Bilingual?
K 20604 Colophon.
K 20605 Omens?
K 20606 Bab. Uncertain. Cf. K 20631?
K 20607 Bab. Letter?
K 20608 Library text.
K 20609 Erra V 32-42.
K 20610 Bulla with stamp seal impression.
K 20611 Illegible.
K 20612 Uncertain.
K 20613 Neo-Assyrian letter.
K 20614 Uncertain.
K 20615 Neo-Assyrian dialect?
K 20616 +K 3061a, prism fragment, royal inscription of Ashurbanipal, dup. Campbell Thompson, *PEA* p. 31 15-17.
K 20617 Uncertain.
K 20618 Uncertain.
K 20619 Uncertain.
K 20620 Astrological omens.
K 20621 Uncertain.
K 20622 Uncertain.
K 20623 Library text.
K 20624 Traces.
K 20625 Bab.
K 20626 Traces.
K 20627 "Rm". +K 20682+20861. Colophon to Tablet II of Emesal Vocabulary (*MSL* IV 26).
K 20628 Dup. Rm II 426 (*BL* 82), Emesal litany.
K 20629 Omens?
K 20630 Uncertain.
K 20631 Bab. Cf. K 20606?
K 20632 Bilingual?
K 20633 Uncertain.
K 20634 Uncertain.
K 20635 Bab. "an.gi$_6$".

K 20636 Omens?
K 20637 "82-5-22". Šamaš Hymn 173-182.
K 20638 +K 9836+, dup. K 10565 and *KAR* 31, bilingual incantation.
K 20639 Sumerian.
K 20640 Fragment of inscribed bulla?
K 20641 Library text.
K 20642 Traces.
K 20643 Traces.
K 20644 Neo-Assyrian legal: conveyance.
K 20645 Administrative?
K 20646 Bab.
K 20647 Uncertain.
K 20648 Rulings only.
K 20649 Uncertain.
K 20650 Omens?
K 20651 Uncertain.
K 20652 Literary ("*raqqu*" and "*šeleppû*")?
K 20653 Omens.
K 20654 Uncertain.
K 20655 Uncertain.
K 20656 Uncertain.
K 20657 Omens?
K 20658 +K 4370+ iii (*MSL* XVII 158), Antagal III 207-211.
K 20659 Library text.
K 20660 Uncertain.
K 20661 Literary/religious.
K 20662 Uncertain.
K 20663 Library text.
K 20664 Uncertain.
K 20665 Uncertain.
K 20666 Omens.
K 20667 Uncertain.
K 20668 Mentions Kulaba.
K 20669 Bilingual incantation.
K 20670 Omens?
K 20671 "Rm". Non-standard *ezibs* from a Neo-Assyrian oracle question (cf. *SAA* IV).
K 20672 "Rm". Uncertain.
K 20673 "Rm". Traces.
K 20674 "Rm". Library text.
K 20675 "Rm". Administrative?
K 20676 "Rm". Library text.
K 20677 "Rm". Fragment of inscribed vessel?
K 20678 "Rm". Literary/religious.
K 20679 "Rm". Astrological omens.
K 20680 "Rm". Ritual.
K 20681 "82-3-23". Literary?
K 20682 +K 20627+, which see.
K 20683 "Rm". Traces.
K 20684 "Rm". Uncertain.
K 20685 "Rm". Inscribed bulla?
K 20686 "Rm". Traces.
K 20687 "Rm". Incantation.
K 20688 "Rm". Uncertain.
K 20689 "Rm". Uncertain.
K 20690 "Rm". Bab. Omens?
K 20691 "Rm". Ashurbanipal colophon.
K 20692 "Rm". Library text.
K 20693 "Rm". Uncertain.
K 20694 "Rm". Ashurbanipal colophon.
K 20695 "Rm". Ashurbanipal colophon.
K 20696 "Rm". Omens?
K 20697 "82-3-23". Lines beginning *ul-la-nu* zi.ga.
K 20698 "Rm". Illegible.
K 20699 "Rm". Ashurbanipal colophon.
K 20700 "Rm". +K 20730. Omens and colophon of Nabû-zuqup-kēna, dated by Ša-Aššur-DuBBu.
K 20701 "Rm". Incantation?
K 20702 "Rm". Magic ritual.
K 20703 "Rm". Ashurbanipal colophon.
K 20704 "Rm". Ashurbanipal colophon.
K 20705 "Rm". Omens.
K 20706 "Rm". Literary/religious.
K 20707 "Rm". God list, dup. *CT* 24 42 98-102.
K 20708 "Rm". Omens.
K 20709 "Rm". Hymn/prayer?
K 20710 "Rm". Literary?
K 20711 "Rm". Uncertain.

K 20712 "Rm". Names of gods with glosses?
K 20713 "Rm". Omens.
K 20714 "Rm". Uncertain.
K 20715 "Rm". Uncertain.
K 20716 "Rm". Ashurbanipal colophon: "tablet XX".
K 20717 "Rm". Uncertain.
K 20718 "Rm". Neo-Assyrian administrative.
K 20719 "Rm". Omens from Ashurbanipal's reign?
K 20720 "Rm". Uncertain.
K 20721 "Rm". Sagalla incantation, dup. *CT* 23 11 37-40; (+)K 7283?
K 20722 "Rm". Uncertain.
K 20723 "Rm". Uncertain.
K 20724 "Rm". Literary/religious.
K 20725 "Rm". Uncertain.
K 20726 Uncertain.
K 20727 "Rm". Uncertain.
K 20728 "Rm". Ashurbanipal colophon.
K 20729 Library text.
K 20730 +K 20700, which see.
K 20731 "Rm". Library text.
K 20732 "Rm". Library text.
K 20733 "Rm". Literary/religious.
K 20734 "Rm". Uncertain.
K 20735 "Rm". Bab. List/litany?
K 20736 "Rm". Colophon.
K 20737 "Rm". Uncertain.
K 20738 "Rm". Bab. Legal/administrative?
K 20739 "Rm". Religious? Part Sumerian.
K 20740 "Rm". Urgud A II or related, dup. *MSL* VIII/2 44 249-253c.
K 20741 "Rm". Uncertain.
K 20742 "Rm". Literary/religious.
K 20743 "Rm". Bilingual, myth?
K 20744 "Rm". Astrological omens?
K 20745 "Rm". Bilingual?
K 20746 "Rm". Library text.
K 20747 "Rm". Topography?
K 20748 "Rm". Uncertain.
K 20749 "Rm". Royal inscription of Ashurbanipal, dup. *VAB* VII 18 78-82.
K 20750 "Rm". Ritual?
K 20751 "Rm". Uncertain.
K 20752 "Rm". Extispicy? Cf. K 20756
K 20753 "Rm". Uncertain.
K 20754 "Rm". Traces on edge.
K 20755 "Rm". Omens.
K 20756 "Rm". Extispicy? Cf. K 20752.
K 20757 "82-3-23". Sumerian litany.
K 20758 "Rm". Traces.
K 20759 "Rm". Library text.
K 20760 "Rm". Library text.
K 20761 "Rm". Library text.
K 20762 "Rm". Library text.
K 20763 "Rm". Omens.
K 20764 "Rm". Uncertain.
K 20765 "Rm". Bab.
K 20766 "Rm". Colophon.
K 20767 "Rm". Literary/religious.
K 20768 "Rm". Traces.
K 20769 "Rm". Omens?
K 20770 "Rm". Complaint psalm.
K 20771 "Rm". Bab. Uncertain.
K 20772 "Rm". Uncertain.
K 20773 "Rm". Uncertain.
K 20774 "Rm". Uncertain.
K 20775 "Rm". Neo-Assyrian administrative (beams).
K 20776 "Rm". Sumerian incantation.
K 20777 "Rm". Litany?
K 20778 "Rm". +K 2756d, Gilgameš I 180-187.
K 20779 "Rm". Library text.
K 20780 "Rm". Uncertain.
K 20781 "Rm". Uncertain.
K 20782 "Rm". Uncertain.
K 20783 "Rm". Bab.
K 20784 "Rm". Personal names?
K 20785 "Rm". Uncertain.
K 20786 "Rm". Ritual or prayer.
K 20787 "Rm". Fragment of *sikkatu*?
K 20788 "Rm". Personal names.

K 20789 "Rm". Uncertain.
K 20790 "Rm". Legal/administrative.
K 20791 "Rm". Legal/administrative.
K 20792 "Rm". Omens.
K 20793 "Rm". Uncertain.
K 20794 "Rm". Uncertain.
K 20795 "Rm". Library text.
K 20796 "Rm". Fragment of *sikkatu*.
K 20797 "Rm". Uncertain.
K 20798 "Rm". Omens?
K 20799 "Rm". Library text.
K 20800 "Rm". Medical.
K 20801 "Rm". Colophon.
K 20802 "82-3-23". Extispicy?
K 20803 "Rm". Magic?
K 20804 "Rm". Religious?
K 20805 "Rm". Religious.
K 20806 "Rm". Hymn.
K 20807 "Rm". Omens?
K 20808 "Rm". Uncertain.
K 20809 "Rm". Uncertain.
K 20810 "Rm". Administrative (wood).
K 20811 "Rm". Literary/religious.
K 20812 "Rm". Traces.
K 20813 "Rm". Sumerian.
K 20814 "Rm". Medical.
K 20815 "Rm". Liver omens, 15th tablet of Multābiltu.
K 20816 "Rm". Literary?
K 20817 "82-3-23". Bab. Akkadian love poetry.
K 20818 "Rm". Uncertain.
K 20819 "Rm". Uncertain.
K 20820 "Rm". "Sippar" or "Euphrates".
K 20821 "Rm". Bab.
K 20822 "Rm". Library text.
K 20823 "Rm". Omens?
K 20824 "Rm". End of library text with colophon.
K 20825 "Rm". List.
K 20826 "Rm". Names of gods.
K 20827 "Rm". Omens?
K 20828 "Rm". Omens?
K 20829 "Rm". Repeated]-*ni-tu-u*.
K 20830 "Rm". Library text.
K 20831 "Rm". Bab. Literary/religious.
K 20832 "Rm". Uncertain.
K 20833 "Rm". Coarse script, traces.
K 20834 "Rm". Administrative?
K 20835 "Rm". Literary?
K 20836 "Rm". Uncertain.
K 20837 "Rm". Uncertain.
K 20838 "Rm". Uncertain.
K 20839 "Rm". Uncertain.
K 20840 "Rm". Uncertain.
K 20841 "Rm". Neo-Assyrian letter?
K 20842 "Rm". Omens.
K 20843 "Rm". Uncertain.
K 20844 "Rm". Omens.
K 20845 "Rm". Magic?
K 20846 "Rm". Bab. Omens?
K 20847 "Rm". Literary?
K 20848 "Rm". Uncertain.
K 20849 "Rm". Uncertain.
K 20850 "Rm". Bilingual.
K 20851 "Rm". Uncertain.
K 20852 "Rm". Uncertain.
K 20853 "Rm". Ashurbanipal colophon.
K 20854 "Rm". Bab. Litany?
K 20855 "Rm". Neo-Assyrian letter.
K 20856 "Rm". Uncertain.
K 20857 "82-3-23". Magic ritual.
K 20858 "Rm". Library text.
K 20859 Traces.
K 20860 "Rm". Astrological omens.
K 20861 +K 20627+, which see.
K 20862 "Rm". Omens.
K 20863 "Rm". Bilingual, cf. *ZA* 40 85 and 88.
K 20864 "Rm". Royal inscription of Sennacherib, third campaign.
K 20865 "Rm". Uncertain.
K 20866 "Rm". Uncertain.
K 20867 "Rm". Bilingual?
K 20868 "Rm". Uncertain.
K 20869 "Rm". Hymn.

K 20870 "Rm". Neo-Assyrian administrative (wood), cf. K 20879.
K 20871 "Rm". Library text.
K 20872 "Rm". Omens.
K 20873 "Rm". Uncertain.
K 20874 "Rm". Library text.
K 20875 "Rm". Bilingual.
K 20876 "Rm". Library text.
K 20877 "Rm". Neo-Assyrian letter.
K 20878 "Rm". Uncertain.
K 20879 "Rm". Neo-Assyrian administrative (wood), cf. K 20870.
K 20880 "Rm". Uncertain.
K 20881 "82-3-23". Literary?
K 20882 "Rm". +K 15320 (+)K 4880, 5134, 5148, bilingual litany, dup. *SBH* p. 134 i 5-12.
K 20883 "Rm". Uncertain.
K 20884 "Rm". Liver omens.
K 20885 "Rm". Uncertain.
K 20886 "Rm". Uncertain.
K 20887 Bab.?
K 20888 Neo-Assyrian letter?
K 20889 Uncertain.
K 20890 Bab. Letter?
K 20891 Bab.
K 20892 Bab.
K 20893 Bab.
K 20894 Uncertain.
K 20895 Uncertain. Cf. K 20896.
K 20896 Uncertain. Cf. K 20985.
K 20897 Bab. Letter.
K 20898 "83-1-18". Bab. Letter.
K 20899 Uncertain.
K 20900 "83-1-18". +83-1-18, 358 (*ADD* 284 = *NALK* 295), Neo-Assyrian legal document.
K 20901 "83-1-18". Bab. Letter.
K 20902 "83-1-18". Bab.
K 20903 "83-1-18". Letter?
K 20904 "83-1-18". Bab. Letter.
K 20905 "83-1-18". Uncertain.
K 20906 "83-1-18". Neo-Assyrian letter.
K 20907 +K 1263 (Parpola, *AOAT* 5/1 279), Neo-Assyrian letter.
K 20908 "83-1-18". Bab. Letter.
K 20909 "83-1-18". Neo-Assyrian letter.
K 20910 "83-1-18". Medical.
K 20911 Uncertain.
K 20912 Bab. Letter?
K 20913 "83-1-18". Uncertain.
K 20914 "83-1-18". Neo-Assyrian letter.
K 20915 "83-1-18". Bab. Letter?
K 20916 "83-1-18". Bab. Letter.
K 20917 "83-1-18". Neo-Assyrian letter.
K 20918 "83-1-18". Omens.
K 20919 "83-1-18". Neo-Assyrian legal, court judgement.
K 20920 "83-1-18". Library text.
K 20921 "83-1-18". Uncertain.
K 20922 "83-1-18". Bilingual incantation.
K 20923 "83-1-18". Omens.
K 20924 "83-1-18". Omens.
K 20925 "83-1-18". Library text.
K 20926 "83-1-18". Emesal, religious.
K 20927 "83-1-18". Omens with commentary, or report.
K 20928 Bab.
K 20929 Uncertain.
K 20930 "83-1-18". Bab. Astrology.
K 20931 "83-1-18". Liver omens.
K 20932 "83-1-18". Library text.
K 20933 "83-1-18". Bab. Uncertain.
K 20934 "83-1-18". Uncertain.
K 20935 "83-1-18". Bab. Letter?
K 20936 "83-1-18". Neo-Assyrian administrative?
K 20937 "83-1-18". Neo-Assyrian letter.
K 20938 "83-1-18". Bab.
K 20939 "83-1-18". Neo-Assyrian legal.
K 20940 "83-1-18". Library text.
K 20941 "83-1-18". Lexical(?) in unusual script.
K 20942 "83-1-18". Bab. Scholarly.
K 20943 Bab. Administrative?

K 20944 "83-1-18". Neo-Assyrian administrative?
K 20945 "83-1-18". Neo-Assyrian legal.
K 20946 Neo-Assyrian letter.
K 20947 "83-1-18". Neo-Assyrian legal?
K 20948 Bab. Religious.
K 20949 "83-1-18". Probably from Sippar. Exercise extracts from Marduk prayer no. 2 and Enūma eliš III.
K 20950 "83-1-18". Ritual?
K 20951 "83-1-18". Neo-Assyrian oracle question (cf. *SAA* IV).
K 20952 Bab. Religious, in part bilingual.
K 20953 "83-1-18". Neo-Assyrian oracle question (cf. *SAA* IV).
K 20954 Names of gods.
K 20955 "83-1-18". Uncertain.
K 20956 "79-7-8". Trace.
K 20957 "83-1-18". Probably from Sippar. Myth involving Ninurta.
K 20958 "83-1-18". Neo-Assyrian administrative, "silver".
K 20959 Coarse Bab. Report?
K 20960 "79-7-8". Bilingual incantation.
K 20961 "79-7-8". List of places.
K 20962 "82-5-22". Mīs pî III? Cf. *STT* 200 39-41 and 70-72.
K 20963 "K". Uncertain.
K 20964 Bab.
K 20965 Uncertain.
K 20966 "Rm II". Uncertain.
K 20967 "Rm II". Library text.
K 20968 Traces and colophon.
K 20969 "Rm II". Incantations.
K 20970 "Rm II". Omens.
K 20971 "Rm II". Bilingual religious.
K 20972 Ashurbanipal colophon.
K 20973 "Rm II". Bab. Royal ritual.
K 20974 "Rm II". Library text.
K 20975 "Rm II". Bilingual incantation and colophon.
K 20976 Literary/religious.
K 20977 "Rm II". Uncertain.
K 20978 "Rm II". Sumerian?
K 20979 Traces.
K 20980 Religious or Neo-Assyrian royal inscription?
K 20981 "Rm II". Omens or administrative.
K 20982 "Rm II". Omens.
K 20983 "Rm II". Bab. Uncertain.
K 20984 "Rm II". Traces and Ashurbanipal colophon.
K 20985 "Rm II". Omens?
K 20986 "Rm II". Ritual?
K 20987 "Rm II". Uncertain.
K 20988 "Rm II". Literary/religious, cf. *KAR* 19 obv.(?) i 11ff.
K 20989 "Rm II". Omens.
K 20990 Šurpu III 150-155?
K 20991 "Rm II". Omens?
K 20992 "Rm II". Uncertain.
K 20993 "Rm II". Ashurbanipal colophon.
K 20994 "Rm II". Litany?
K 20995 Omens.
K 20996 "Rm II". Astrological omens.
K 20997 Ashurbanipal colophon.
K 20998 "Rm II". Bulla with stamp seal impression.
K 20999 Colophon: "Total 48 [...".
K 21000 "Rm II". Uncertain.
K 21001 "Rm II". Uncertain.
K 21002 "Rm II". Illegible.
K 21003 "Rm II". Uncertain.
K 21004 +K 21006. Astrological omens (*attalû*), dup. Rochberg-Halton, *AfO* Beiheft 22 pp. 263-265.
K 21005 Administrative?
K 21006 +K 21004, which see.
K 21007 "Rm II". Literary/religious.
K 21008 "Rm II". Library text.
K 21009 Uncertain.
K 21010 "Rm II". Colophon.
K 21011 "Rm II". Uncertain.
K 21012 "Rm II". Same colophon as K 21010.

K 21013 "Rm II". Omens?
K 21014 "Rm II". Commentary ("*mukallimtu*").
K 21015 "Rm II". Medical.
K 21016 "Rm II". Omens.
K 21017 "Rm II". Omens (Šumma ālu?).
K 21018 "Rm II". Uncertain.
K 21019 "Rm II". Bab. Omens from crows (*āribu*).
K 21020 "Rm II". Uncertain.
K 21021 "Rm II". Omens (Šumma ālu?).
K 21022 "Rm II". Library text.
K 21023 "Rm II". Omens.
K 21024 "Rm II". Neo-Assyrian administrative.
K 21025 "Rm II". Neo-Assyrian legal?
K 21026 Omens.
K 21027 "Rm II". Library text?
K 21028 "Rm II". Bab. Library text.
K 21029 "Rm". Incantations and rituals.
K 21030 Bab. Names of temples. Litany?
K 21031 "82-3-23". +K 2014+, Urra=ḫubullu V 169-176 (*MSL* VI 20).
K 21032 Bilingual incantation.
K 21033 Omens.
K 21034 "Rm II". Neo-Assyrian letter.
K 21035 "82-3-23". Bab. Letter of scholar.
K 21036 "Rm". Traces.
K 21037 "Rm II". Library text.
K 21038 "Rm". Traces.
K 21039 "Rm II". Traces.
K 21040 "Rm II". Library text.
K 21041 "Rm". Uncertain.
K 21042 "Rm". Uncertain.
K 21043 "Rm". Neo-Assyrian legal.
K 21044 Neo-Assyrian legal.
K 21045 "Rm II". Uncertain.
K 21046 "Rm II". Traces.
K 21047 "Rm II". Omens, administrative or lexical.
K 21048 "Rm II". Literary/religious.
K 21049 "Rm II". Neo-Assyrian letter.
K 21050 "Rm II". Large script.
K 21051 "Rm II". Colophon, "Second [*nisḫu*]".
K 21052 "Rm II". Lexical.
K 21053 "Rm II". Bab. Library text.
K 21054 "Rm II". Library text.
K 21055 "Rm II". Omens, administrative or lexical.
K 21056 "Rm II, III"! Omens, prophecies?
K 21057 "Rm II, III"! Library text.
K 21058 "Rm II, III"! Colophon.
K 21059 "Rm II, III"! Literary/religious or omens?
K 21060 "Rm II, III"! Uncertain.
K 21061 Uncertain.
K 21062 Bab.
K 21063 "81-2-4". Bab. Omens.
K 21064 "82-3-23". Library text.
K 21065 "81-2-4". Omens.
K 21066 "81-2-4". Uncertain.
K 21067 "81-2-4". Colophon.
K 21068 "81-2-4". Bab. Colophon?
K 21069 "81-2-4". Syllabary A 232-239 (*MSL* III 30) in archaizing sign forms.
K 21070 "81-2-4". Neo-Assyrian letter.
K 21071 "81-2-4". Dream incantations and rituals.
K 21072 "81-2-4". Bab. Anzû II 47-55, 120-128; (+)K 3008 (+)K 18740 (+)K 19368
K 21073 "81-2-4". Hymn or royal inscription?
K 21074 "81-2-4". Bab. Religious, names of Zarpānītum.
K 21075 "81-2-4". Administrative?
K 21076 Liver omens.
K 21077 "81-2-4". Bab. Letter?
K 21078 "81-2-4". Sumerian, religious.
K 21079 "81-2-4". Bab. Bilingual?
K 21080 "81-2-4". Neo-Assyrian oracle question (cf. *SAA* IV).
K 21081 "81-2-4". Uncertain.

K 21082 “81-2-4”. Uncertain.
K 21083 “81-2-4”. Prayer to Šamaš?
K 21084 “81-2-4”. Religious?
K 21085 “81-2-4”. Library text.
K 21086 “81-2-4”. Bab.
K 21087 “81-2-4”. Omens.
K 21088 “81-2-4”. Uncertain.
K 21089 “81-2-4”. Omens.
K 21090 “81-2-4”. Bilingual.
K 21091 “81-2-4”. Bab. Omens?
K 21092 “81-2-4”. Uninscribed piece of vessel (*sikkatu*?).
K 21093 “81-2-4”. Uncertain.
K 21094 “81-2-4”. Sumerian incantations.
K 21095 “81-2-4”. Uncertain.
K 21096 “81-2-4”. Bilingual, Cassite or II Isin?
K 21097 “81-2-4”. Uncertain.
K 21098 “81-2-4”. Uncertain.
K 21099 “81-2-4”. Neo-Assyrian letter.
K 21100 “81-2-4”. Prayer?
K 21101 “81-2-4”. Prayer or letter?
K 21102 “81-2-4”. Uncertain.
K 21103 “81-2-4”. Neo-Assyrian legal.
K 21104 “81-2-4”. Library text.
K 21105 “81-2-4”. Neo-Assyrian legal?
K 21106 “81-2-4”. Neo-Assyrian letter.
K 21107 “81-2-4”. Library text?
K 21108 “81-2-4”. Large, coarse script.
K 21109 “81-2-4”. Ashurbanipal colophon.
K 21110 “81-2-4”. Neo-Assyrian legal? Cf. K 21103.
K 21111 “81-2-4”. Omens.
K 21112 “81-2-4”. Administrative.
K 21113 “81-2-4”. Omens? Cf. K 21137.
K 21114 “82-3-23”. Bab. Letter.
K 21115 “81-2-4”. Omens?
K 21116 “82-3-23”. Bab. Astrological omens?
K 21117 Literary?
K 21118 “81-2-4”. Bab. Uncertain.
K 21119 Fragment of Old Babylonian cylinder: lexical?
K 21120 Incantations.
K 21121 Traces.
K 21122 Liver omens.
K 21123 Uncertain.
K 21124 Colophon.
K 21125 Ashurbanipal colophon.
K 21126 Bilingual.
K 21127 Bab. Hymn or prayer.
K 21128 Uncertain.
K 21129 Bab. Letter?
K 21130 Neo-Assyrian letter?
K 21131 Scholarly text.
K 21132 Sumerian.
K 21133 Uncertain.
K 21134 Astrological omens.
K 21135 Library text.
K 21136 Uncertain.
K 21137 Omens? Cf. K 21113.
K 21138 Uncertain.
K 21139 Omens.
K 21140 Coarse script. Neo-Assyrian letter?
K 21141 Stars.
K 21142 Uncertain.
K 21143 Sumerian.
K 21144 Scholarly text.
K 21145 Bilingual hymn?
K 21146 Astrological omens.
K 21147 Uncertain.
K 21148 Omens.
K 21149 Uncertain.
K 21150 Liver omens.
K 21151 Omens.
K 21152 Uncertain.
K 21153 Omens.
K 21154 Colophon?
K 21155 Neo-Assyrian legal?
K 21156 Library text.
K 21157 Omens?
K 21158 Uncertain.
K 21159 Omens?
K 21160 Uncertain.
K 21161 Bilingual incantation.

K 21162 Colophon.
K 21163 Lexical?
K 21164 Uncertain.
K 21165 Uncertain.
K 21166 Uncertain.
K 21167 Uncertain.
K 21168 Uncertain.
K 21169 Omens.
K 21170 Ritual.
K 21171 Uncertain.
K 21172 Library text.
K 21173 Uncertain.
K 21174 Ritual?
K 21175 Traces.
K 21176 Uncertain.
K 21177 Omens.
K 21178 Omens.
K 21179 Bab. Bilingual Eršaḫunga.
K 21180 Coarse script.
K 21181 Uncertain.
K 21182 Medical?
K 21183 Administrative?
K 21184 Ritual.
K 21185 Izi-išātu H 184-191 (*MSL* XIII 207).
K 21186 Omens.
K 21187 Library text.
K 21188 Religious, names Ea and Zarpānītum.
K 21189 Library text.
K 21190 +K 4900+, see K 17627.
K 21191 Omens.
K 21192 Colophon.
K 21193 Ritual.
K 21194 Bab.
K 21195 Uncertain.
K 21196 Uncertain.
K 21197 Colophon?
K 21198 Omens.
K 21199 Library text.
K 21200 Extispicy.
K 21201 Bab. Legal.
K 21202 Sumerian?
K 21203 Library text.
K 21204 Omens?
K 21205 Neo-Assyrian letter?
K 21206 Traces.
K 21207 Odd signs.
K 21208 Uncertain.
K 21209 Names of gods.
K 21210 Uncertain.
K 21211 Bilingual.
K 21212 Omens.
K 21213 Uncertain.
K 21214 Uncertain.
K 21215 Literary/religious?
K 21216 Traces.
K 21217 Omens?
K 21218 Uncertain.
K 21219 Library text.
K 21220 Coarse script.
K 21221 Bilingual.
K 21222 Library text.
K 21223 Library text.
K 21224 Uncertain.
K 21225 Ritual.
K 21226 Neo-Assyrian letter?
K 21227 Laws of Hammurabi?
K 21228 Uncertain.
K 21229 Bab. Omens.
K 21230 Incantation.
K 21231 Literary?
K 21232 Traces.
K 21233 Uncertain.
K 21234 Medical?
K 21235 Astrological omens?
K 21236 Bilingual incantation.
K 21237 Uncertain.
K 21238 Uncertain.
K 21239 Uncertain.
K 21240 Colophon.
K 21241 Literary/religious.
K 21242 Uncertain.
K 21243 Incantation or related ritual?
K 21244 Traces.
K 21245 Uncertain.
K 21246 The sign bàd glossed ba-ad.
K 21247 Library text?

K 21248 Traces.
K 21249 Prayer.
K 21250 Library text.
K 21251 Omens.
K 21252 Liver omens.
K 21253 Uncertain.
K 21254 Colophon.
K 21255 Library text.
K 21256 Traces.
K 21257 Religious/literary?
K 21258 Uncertain.
K 21259 Library text.
K 21260 Medical.
K 21261 Uncertain.
K 21262 Omens.
K 21263 Omens?
K 21264 Legal/administrative?
K 21265 Uncertain.
K 21266 Library text.
K 21267 Coarse script.
K 21268 Uncertain.
K 21269 Uncertain.
K 21270 Traces.
K 21271 Uncertain.
K 21272 Omens?
K 21273 Omens?
K 21274 Uncertain.
K 21275 Uncertain.
K 21276 Uncertain.
K 21277 Library text.
K 21278 Uncertain.
K 21279 Omens.
K 21280 Omens?
K 21281 Uncertain.
K 21282 Library text.
K 21283 Uncertain.
K 21284 Bab. Letter?
K 21285 Uncertain.
K 21286 Administrative?
K 21287 Bab. Literary/religious?
K 21288 Uncertain.
K 21289 Uncertain.
K 21290 Lexical?
K 21291 Bab. Library text.
K 21292 Bilingual?
K 21293 Marduk's Address?
K 21294 a. Fragment of envelope.
K 21294 b. Neo-Assyrian legal, conveyance.
K 21295 Uncertain.
K 21296 Omens.
K 21297 Uncertain.
K 21298 Literary/religious.
K 21299 Bab.?
K 21300 Literary/religious?
K 21301 Uncertain.
K 21302 Uncertain.
K 21303 Uncertain.
K 21304 Coarse script.
K 21305 Literary/religious?
K 21306 Neo-Babylonian letter?
K 21307 Library text.
K 21308 Uncertain.
K 21309 Library text?
K 21310 Library text.
K 21311 Uncertain.
K 21312 Omens.
K 21313 Omens.
K 21314 Library text.
K 21315 Uncertain.
K 21316 Literary or Neo-Assyrian royal inscription?
K 21317 Uncertain.
K 21318 Uncertain.
K 21319 Astrological.
K 21320 Neo-Assyrian legal, field conveyance.
K 21321 Uncertain.
K 21322 Neo-Assyrian letter?
K 21323 Uncertain.
K 21324 Omens.
K 21325 Literary or royal inscription?
K 21326 Unusual Neo-Assyrian script.
K 21327 Uncertain.
K 21328 Tamītu?
K 21329 Library text.
K 21330 Uncertain.
K 21331 Library text.

K 21332 Uncertain.
K 21333 Uncertain.
K 21334 Uncertain.
K 21335 Colophon.
K 21336 Bab. Omens.
K 21337 Uncertain.
K 21338 Uncertain.
K 21339 Medical.
K 21340 Omens.
K 21341 Uncertain.
K 21342 Colophon?
K 21343 Uncertain.
K 21344 List of names of gods?
K 21345 Religious.
K 21346 Uncertain.
K 21347 Uncertain.
K 21348 Uncertain.
K 21349 Uncertain.
K 21350 Library text?
K 21351 Uncertain.
K 21352 Uncertain.
K 21353 Illegible.
K 21354 Literary/religious?
K 21355 Library text?
K 21356 Library text.
K 21357 Uncertain.
K 21358 Library text.
K 21359 Library text.
K 21360 Neo-Assyrian letter.
K 21361 Uncertain.
K 21362 Uncertain.
K 21363 Neo-Assyrian letter?
K 21364 Uncertain.
K 21365 Uncertain.
K 21366 Uncertain.
K 21367 Uncertain.
K 21368 Uncertain.
K 21369 Library text.
K 21370 Omens?
K 21371 Uncertain.
K 21372 Uncertain.
K 21373 Bab.
K 21374 Neo-Babylonian letter?
K 21375 Traces.
K 21376 Traces.
K 21377 Neo-Assyrian royal inscription?
K 21378 Uncertain.
K 21379 "82-3-23". Bilingual litany beginning é.kur.ta.
K 21380 Library text.
K 21381 Uncertain.
K 21382 Library text?
K 21383 +K 5007+...21384, see K 18643.
K 21384 See K 21383.
K 21385 Exorcistic.
K 21386 +K 5343, bilingual Šuilla for Nanna (Sjöberg, *Mondgott* 168 27-31), cf. K 8416.
K 21387 Library text.
K 21388 +K 7602+, bilingual incantation, dup. *AOAT* I 10 196-200.
K 21389 +K 21813 (+)K 21417, royal inscription of Ashurbanipal, dup. *VAB* VII p. 14 6-13.
K 21390 List of temple names?
K 21391 Love poetry.
K 21392 Witchcraft.
K 21393 (+)Sm 398, prayer to Nergal (*UFBG* p. 402).
K 21394 +K 2526+, Bīt rimki, House III A.
K 21395 +K 56+, Ana ittišu IV i 50-58 (*MSL* I 54-55).
K 21396 (+)K 3054+, Udugḫul XIII, dup. *AAA* 22 76 27-34.
K 21397 Library text.
K 21398 Literary/religious.
K 21399 Ritual, dup. *BBR* 1-20 39-47, (+)K 3242+ (+)K 5785+ (+)K 10917+? Cf. K 21499.
K 21400 Sumerian incantation.
K 21401 Sumerian or bilingual.
K 21402 Library text?
K 21403 Sumerian.
K 21404 Bilingual.
K 21405 Lines beginning *lu-u*.

K 21406 +K 4170+, Urra=ḫubullu I 154-159 (*MSL* V 19-20).
K 21407 Bilingual.
K 21408 Omens, about a bed.
K 21409 Uncertain.
K 21410 Uncertain.
K 21411 Bilingual.
K 21412 +K 3890+, Šurpu VIII 69-73, see K 17045.
K 21413 Sumerian litany.
K 21414 Library text.
K 21415 Emesal litany, cf. K 21425.
K 21416 Bilingual exorcistic.
K 21417 (+)K 21389+, which see. Dup. *VAB* VII p. 14 3-8.
K 21418 Prayer to Ištar of Nineveh, dup. K 20+ 1-6 (*AfO* XI pl. vi p. 368).
K 21419 Library text.
K 21420 Royal inscription of Ashurbanipal, dup. *VAB* VII p. 16 37-41, etc.
K 21421 (+)K 4562+, Emesal Vocabulary I 32-35 (*MSL* IV 6).
K 21422 Hymn?
K 21423 Bilingual.
K 21424 Sumerian.
K 21425 Emesal litany, cf. K 21415
K 21426 Prayer.
K 21427 God list or exorcism?
K 21428 Uncertain.
K 21429 Temple names.
K 21430 Library text.
K 21431 Incantation?
K 21432 Bilingual incantation, dup. *CT* 16 10 V?
K 21433 List of names of gods.
K 21434 (+)K 4317+, Ana ittišu VI iv 46-50 (*MSL* I p. 89). Cf. K 22163.
K 21435 Uncertain.
K 21436 Abraded.
K 21437 Piece of envelope with impression of Neo-Assyrian royal type stamp seal.
K 21438 Uncertain.
K 21439 Library text.
K 21440 Library text.
K 21441 Large Bab.
K 21442 Uncertain.
K 21443 Bab. Letter?
K 21444 Traces and Ashurbanipal colophon.
K 21445 Traces.
K 21446 Library text.
K 21447 Literary/religious.
K 21448 Uncertain.
K 21449 Uncertain.
K 21450 Library text.
K 21451 Uncertain.
K 21452 Repeated *idû*(?).
K 21453 Uncertain.
K 21454 Traces.
K 21455 Small oblong tablet.
K 21456 Uncertain.
K 21457 Uncertain.
K 21458 Colophon.
K 21459 Illegible.
K 21460 Traces.
K 21461 Administrative.
K 21462 Uncertain.
K 21463 Traces.
K 21464 Uncertain.
K 21465 Uncertain.
K 21466 Omens?
K 21467 Bab. Literary/religious.
K 21468 Bab.
K 21469 Uncertain.
K 21470 Uncertain.
K 21471 Uncertain.
K 21472 Uncertain.
K 21473 Uncertain.
K 21474 Uncertain.
K 21475 Uncertain.
K 21476 Bab.
K 21477 Uncertain.
K 21478 Royal ritual?

K 21479 Dup. *AKA* pp. 40-41 ii 24-31, royal inscription of Tiglath-pileser I.
K 21480 Uncertain.
K 21481 Astrological(?) omens.
K 21482 Uncertain.
K 21483 Library text?
K 21484 Omens?
K 21485 Neo-Assyrian administrative?
K 21486 Uncertain.
K 21487 Sumerian or bilingual?
K 21488 Liver omens?
K 21489 Library text.
K 21490 Uncertain.
K 21491 Uncertain.
K 21492 Omens.
K 21493 Sumerian?
K 21494 Bab. Library text.
K 21495 Uncertain.
K 21496 Administrative or legal?
K 21497 Literary.
K 21498 Library text.
K 21499 Cf. K 21399?
K 21500 Uncertain.
K 21501 Bilingual?
K 21502 +K 8594+, Gilgameš XI 147-153, Haupt, *Nimrod-Epos* p. 125 no. 65*.
K 21503 Administrative?
K 21504 Omens?
K 21505 Bab.
K 21506 Uncertain.
K 21507 Uncertain.
K 21508 Omens?
K 21509 Literary/religious?
K 21510 Uncertain.
K 21511 Prism fragment.
K 21512 Library text.
K 21513 Omens?
K 21514 Omens.
K 21515 Uncertain.
K 21516 Uncertain.
K 21517 Omens?
K 21518 Traces.
K 21519 Bab.
K 21520 Bab. Literary/religious.
K 21521 Omens?
K 21522 Bab.
K 21523 Literary/religious.
K 21524 Uncertain.
K 21525 Prayer?
K 21526 Uncertain.
K 21527 Uncertain.
K 21528 Bab. Omens?
K 21529 Uncertain.
K 21530 Uncertain.
K 21531 Bab.
K 21532 Library text.
K 21533 Uncertain.
K 21534 Uncertain.
K 21535 Names Ashurbanipal.
K 21536 Administrative?
K 21537 Bab.
K 21538 Traces.
K 21539 Omens.
K 21540 Exorcistic?
K 21541 Uncertain.
K 21542 Tamītu, cf. DT 144.
K 21543 Sumerian.
K 21544 Medical.
K 21545 Uncertain.
K 21546 Library text.
K 21547 Uncertain.
K 21548 Uncertain.
K 21549 Administrative?
K 21550 Uncertain.
K 21551 Uncertain.
K 21552 Uncertain.
K 21553 Traces.
K 21554 Library text.
K 21555 Administrative?
K 21556 Uncertain.
K 21557 Uncertain.
K 21558 Uncertain.
K 21559 Library text.
K 21560 Literary/letter?
K 21561 Bab.
K 21562 Uncertain.

K 21563 Library text?
K 21564 Uncertain.
K 21565 Uncertain.
K 21566 Library text.
K 21567 Library text.
K 21568 List of Akkadian words.
K 21569 Library text.
K 21570 Uncertain.
K 21571 Uncertain.
K 21572 Omens?
K 21573 Library text?
K 21574 Uncertain.
K 21575 Library text.
K 21576 Uncertain.
K 21577 Library text.
K 21578 Bab. Letter.
K 21579 Uncertain.
K 21580 Omens?
K 21581 Library text.
K 21582 Neo-Assyrian letter?
K 21583 Akkadian Šu'illa, dup. BM 134774; (+)BM 122646. See W. R. Mayer, *Or.* 59 470f.
K 21584 Uncertain.
K 21585 Neo-Assyrian royal inscription?
K 21586 Bilingual.
K 21587 Library text.
K 21588 Library text.
K 21589 Tamītu?
K 21590 Bab. Library text.
K 21591 Omens.
K 21592 Uncertain.
K 21593 Uncertain.
K 21594 Literary/religious.
K 21595 Library text.
K 21596 +K 1621a+, royal inscription of Tiglath-pileser I, dup. *AKA* 52 iii 36-39.
K 21597 Bab. Library text.
K 21598 "83-1-18". Liver omens.
K 21599 Uncertain.
K 21600 Uncertain.
K 21601 Neo-Assyrian administrative?
K 21602 Library text.
K 21603 Uncertain.
K 21604 Library text.
K 21605 Uncertain.
K 21606 Library text.
K 21607 Library text.
K 21608 "K". Medical.
K 21609 Bab. Omens or letter?
K 21610 Colophon?
K 21611 Library text.
K 21612 Omens.
K 21613 Uncertain.
K 21614 Physiognomic omens.
K 21615 Bab.
K 21616 Uncertain.
K 21617 Library text.
K 21618 Uncertain.
K 21619 Uncertain.
K 21620 "K". Neo-Assyrian letter.
K 21621 Bab.
K 21622 Library text.
K 21623 Bab. Ritual?
K 21624 Bab. Omens.
K 21625 Library text.
K 21626 Bab. Omens, dup. *ACh* Supp. 2 Ištar LXXIII 11-15.
K 21627 Uncertain.
K 21628 Literary/religious.
K 21629 Library text?
K 21630 Omens.
K 21631 Uncertain.
K 21632 Uncertain.
K 21633 Bab.?
K 21634 Uncertain.
K 21635 Uncertain.
K 21636 Library text.
K 21637 Bab.
K 21638 Uncertain.
K 21639 Bab.
K 21640 Uncertain.
K 21641 Bab. Omens.
K 21642 Uncertain.
K 21643 Uncertain.
K 21644 Neo-Assyrian letter?
K 21645 Bab. Literary/religious?

K 21646 "K". Library text.
K 21647 Uncertain.
K 21648 Litany?
K 21649 Library text.
K 21650 Uncertain.
K 21651 Literary/royal inscription?
K 21652 Uncertain.
K 21653 Bab. Incantation prayer to Marduk.
K 21654 Sumerian?
K 21655 Neo-Assyrian letter?
K 21656 Uncertain.
K 21657 "K". Emesal litany/prayer.
K 21658 Neo-Assyrian letter?
K 21659 Uncertain.
K 21660 Library text.
K 21661 Omens?
K 21662 Exorcistic.
K 21663 Omens.
K 21664 An=Anum III 155-161.
K 21665 Administrative/tribute list?
K 21666 Omens?
K 21667 Snake omens, cf. *CT* 38 36 77-78.
K 21668 Omens?
K 21669 Extispicy?
K 21670 Omens.
K 21671 Omens?
K 21672 Royal inscription of Ashurbanipal, dup. *VAB* VII 114 34-40.
K 21673 Library text.
K 21674 Tamītu, dup. DT 144.
K 21675 Omens.
K 21676 Library text.
K 21677 Uncertain.
K 21678 Bilingual?
K 21679 Uncertain.
K 21680 Bilingual?
K 21681 Omens.
K 21682 Omens.
K 21683 Omens.
K 21684 Medical.
K 21685 Bab. Literary/religious.
K 21686 Bab. Omens.
K 21687 Bab. Omens.
K 21688 Neo-Assyrian letter?
K 21689 Bab. Incantation.
K 21690 Omens.
K 21691 Uncertain.
K 21692 Uncertain.
K 21693 Bab. Omens?
K 21694 Literary/religious.
K 21695 Library text.
K 21696 Uncertain.
K 21697 Omens.
K 21698 Litany?
K 21699 Omens?
K 21700 "K". Omens?
K 21701 Bab. Bilingual, lexical?
K 21702 Bab. Letter(?) mentioning a tablet of Šumma ālu.
K 21703 Uncertain.
K 21704 Bilingual.
K 21705 Omens from reeds (Šumma ālu LXII?).
K 21706 Library text.
K 21707 Library text.
K 21708 Bab. Letter.
K 21709 Bab. Traces.
K 21710 Omens.
K 21711 Bab. Letter.
K 21712 Library text.
K 21713 Bilingual.
K 21714 +K 3138+ (*JCS* 21 5 41-43) Bīt rimki, House III.
K 21715 Omens.
K 21716 Uncertain.
K 21717 Bab. Cf. K 21815.
K 21718 Bab.
K 21719 Uncertain.
K 21720 Uncertain.
K 21721 Uncertain.
K 21722 Uncertain.
K 21723 Uncertain.
K 21724 Sumerian?
K 21725 Lexical or administrative.
K 21726 "K". Sumerian?

K 21727 Uncertain.
K 21728 Omens?
K 21729 Uncertain.
K 21730 Omens?
K 21731 Library text.
K 21732 Library text?
K 21733 Uncertain.
K 21734 Omens.
K 21735 "K". Bab.
K 21736 Bab. Letter.
K 21737 Uncertain.
K 21738 Library text.
K 21739 Library text.
K 21740 Uncertain.
K 21741 Sumerian?
K 21742 Uncertain.
K 21743 Omens.
K 21744 Repeated *šu-ur*.
K 21745 Bab.
K 21746 Omens.
K 21747 Bilingual?
K 21748 Uncertain.
K 21749 Library text.
K 21750 Uncertain.
K 21751 Sumerian?
K 21752 Library text.
K 21753 Bilingual.
K 21754 Uncertain.
K 21755 +K 16958, which see.
K 21756 Uncertain.
K 21757 Omens?
K 21758 Royal inscription of Tiglath-pileser I, dup. *AKA* p. 76 83-87.
K 21759 Administrative?
K 21760 Uncertain.
K 21761 Omens.
K 21762 Dup. *CT* 16 9 i 23-26, Udugḫul IV. Cf. K 17391.
K 21763 Colophon.
K 21764 Uncertain.
K 21765 Bab.
K 21766 Sumerian?
K 21767 "K". Omens or administrative?
K 21768 Bab.
K 21769 Bab.
K 21770 "K". Uncertain.
K 21771 Uncertain.
K 21772 Uncertain.
K 21773 Religious.
K 21774 Literary/religious?
K 21775 Uncertain.
K 21776 Uncertain.
K 21777 Omens.
K 21778 Library text.
K 21779 Bilingual?
K 21780 Repeated lú.maḫ.
K 21781 Bab.
K 21782 Library text.
K 21783 Library text.
K 21784 Traces.
K 21785 Uncertain.
K 21786 Library text.
K 21787 Repeated šilam.
K 21788 Administrative?
K 21789 Uncertain.
K 21790 Uncertain.
K 21791 Library text.
K 21792 Bab.
K 21793 Uncertain.
K 21794 Colophon.
K 21795 Colophon.
K 21796 Library text?
K 21797 Library text.
K 21798 Religious.
K 21799 Uncertain.
K 21800 Uncertain.
K 21801 Lexical: archaic sign forms?
K 21802 Sumerian.
K 21803 Bab. Bilingual.
K 21804 Bab.
K 21805 Omens?
K 21806 Omens.
K 21807 Ashurbanipal colophon.
K 21808 Library text.
K 21809 Neo-Assyrian letter.
K 21810 Uncertain.
K 21811 Library text.
K 21812 Exposition of temple names.

K 21813 +K 21389, which see.
K 21814 Bilingual.
K 21815 Bab. Cf. K 21717.
K 21816 Literary/religious.
K 21817 Library text.
K 21818 Omens.
K 21819 "K". Sumerian or omens?
K 21820 List of plant names.
K 21821 Library text.
K 21822 Religious.
K 21823 Uncertain.
K 21824 List of stone names?
K 21825 Large script, Neo-Assyrian content.
K 21826 Literary/religious.
K 21827 Uncertain.
K 21828 Names Eridu.
K 21829 Library text.
K 21830 Library text.
K 21831 Bab. Exorcism?
K 21832 Uncertain.
K 21833 Prayer?
K 21834 Uncertain.
K 21835 Neo-Assyrian legal/administrative.
K 21836 Library text.
K 21837 Uncertain.
K 21838 Uncertain.
K 21839 Bab.
K 21840 Uncertain.
K 21841 Bab. Letter?
K 21842 Uncertain.
K 21843 Uncertain.
K 21844 Uncertain.
K 21845 "K". Uncertain.
K 21846 Uncertain.
K 21847 +K 4918+ (*STC* I 180), bilingual incantation.
K 21848 Bilingual.
K 21849 Uncertain.
K 21850 Sumerian or bilingual.
K 21851 +K 3399+ obv. ii-iii, Atra-ḫasīs I, D. Charpin and F. Joannès (eds.), *Marchands, diplomates et empereurs* pp. 411-414*.
K 21852 Colophon.
K 21853 Library text.
K 21854 Incipits(?) of omen tablets (Šumma ālu).
K 21855 (+)K 5211, bilingual incantation, dup. *CT* 13 37.
K 21856 +K 13865, Enūma eliš VI 150-155, probably (+)K 12000b+.
K 21857 Emesal or bilingual.
K 21858 +K 21905. Medical.
K 21859 Ashurbanipal colophon.
K 21860 Bab. Omens.
K 21861 Uncertain.
K 21862 Literary/religious?
K 21863 Literary?
K 21864 Literary/religious?
K 21865 Uncertain.
K 21866 Bab. Prayer.
K 21867 Plant list or literary?
K 21868 Literary?
K 21869 Impression of stamp seal: god standing in crescent.
K 21870 Bab. Letter? Cf. K 21906, 21938.
K 21871 Neo-Assyrian letter.
K 21872 Omens.
K 21873 Ashurbanipal colophon.
K 21874 Uncertain.
K 21875 Bilingual.
K 21876 Literary/religious.
K 21877 Literary/religious.
K 21878 "82-3-23". Uncertain.
K 21879 Literary/religious
K 21880 Literary prayer.
K 21881 Literary/religious
K 21882 "K". Medical.
K 21883 Astrology?
K 21884 Uncertain.
K 21885 Bab. Letter?
K 21886 "82-5-22". Neo-Assyrian administrative.
K 21887 Literary/religious.

K 21888 "82-3-23". Ashurbanipal colophon.
K 21889 +K 10661, Šarrat Nippuri hymn III 57-62 (*Zikir šumim* p. 198).
K 21890 (+)K 8665+? Malku=šarru I 205-210 (*JAOS* 83 428).
K 21891 Library text.
K 21892 Library text.
K 21893 +K 4411+, Urgud to Urra=ḫubullu X (*MSL* VII 114) 136-141.
K 21894 Šumma ālu.
K 21895 Omens.
K 21896 Bilingual?
K 21897 (+)K 2266+? Dream omens, cf. Oppenheim, *Dreams* pp. 314ff.
K 21898 Literary or omens?
K 21899 Uncertain.
K 21900 "82-3-23". Ritual?
K 21901 "82-3-23". Literary/religious.
K 21902 Bab. Library text.
K 21903 Bab. Library text.
K 21904 Library text.
K 21905 See K 21858.
K 21906 Bab. Letter. Cf. K 21870, 21938.
K 21907 Literary/religious.
K 21908 Neo-Assyrian prism. Royal inscription?
K 21909 Bab. Exorcistic.
K 21910 Library text.
K 21911 Omens.
K 21912 Bab. Omens.
K 21913 Astrological omens, cf. *ACh* Adad XII-XV.
K 21914 Prayer?
K 21915 Library text.
K 21916 Omens?
K 21917 Omens?
K 21918 Literary/religious?
K 21919 Library text.
K 21920 Bab. Literary?
K 21921 Astrology?
K 21922 "82-3-23". Bab. Religious?
K 21923 "82-3-23". Bab. Letter.
K 21924 Religious?
K 21925 "82-5-22". Omens.
K 21926 "82-5-22". Prayer to a plurality of gods.
K 21927 Medical omens from the toes, cf. *TDP* p. 144.
K 21928 "82-3-23". Omens.
K 21929 "82-3-23". Extispicy. Coarse script.
K 21930 Uncertain.
K 21931 Omens?
K 21932 Omens.
K 21933 "82-5-22". Bab.
K 21934 Library text.
K 21935 "82-3-23". Library text.
K 21936 Omens.
K 21937 "82-5-22". Bab. Omens.
K 21938 Bab. Letter. Cf. K 21870, 21906.
K 21939 Library text.
K 21940 Uncertain.
K 21941 Bab. Uncertain.
K 21942 Bab. Religious?
K 21943 Omens.
K 21944 Omens.
K 21945 Bab. Omens.
K 21946 Šumma ālu.
K 21947 Omens.
K 21948 Bab. Letter?
K 21949 Late Babylonian administrative?
K 21950 "82-3-23". Neo-Assyrian letter?
K 21951 Neo-Assyrian letter?
K 21952 Omens?
K 21953 Library text.
K 21954 Šumma izbu.
K 21955 Omens?
K 21956 Bab.
K 21957 (+)K 2016a rev. vi, Urra=ḫubullu IV 422-428 (*MSL* V 185).
K 21958 Hymn.
K 21959 Omens.
K 21960 Bilingual exorcism.

K 21961 "K". Library text.
K 21962 "82-3-23". Oblong tablet. Omens?
K 21963 "82-3-23". Ashurbanipal colophon.
K 21964 Library text.
K 21965 Bab. Ritual.
K 21966 Medical?
K 21967 Extispicy?
K 21968 "80-7-19". Library text.
K 21969 Bilingual, religious.
K 21970 Neo-Assyrian administrative.
K 21971 "82-3-23". Bab. Administrative or legal?
K 21972 Temples?
K 21973 (+)K 9022+, Ḫulbazizi 52-57.
K 21974 "82-3-23". Bab. Prayers.
K 21975 "82-3-23". Bab. Administrative?
K 21976 "82-5-22". Religious.
K 21977 Lexical?
K 21978 Bab. Religious?
K 21979 Library text.
K 21980 Ritual.
K 21981 Uncertain.
K 21982 "82-5-22". Neo-Assyrian letter.
K 21983 (+)K 1620a, royal inscription of Tiglath-pileser I, *AKA* p. 78 v 99-vi 4.
K 21984 Bab. Letter?
K 21985 Medical.
K 21986 Medical?
K 21987 Ashurbanipal colophon.
K 21988 Library text.
K 21989 Astrological omens, cf. K 2310, 2894+.
K 21990 "82-3-23". "... silver ... cornelian ...".
K 21991 Uncertain.
K 21992 Neo-Assyrian administrative?
K 21993 Incantation and ritual.
K 21994 Bab. Uncertain.
K 21995 Omens.
K 21996 Literary/religious
K 21997 Bab. Library text.
K 21998 Library text.
K 21999 Bab. Omens.
K 22000 Library text.
K 22001 Literary/royal inscription?
K 22002 Neo-Assyrian letter
K 22003 Bab. Letter?
K 22004 Library text.
K 22005 Bab. Letter?
K 22006 Bab. Uncertain.
K 22007 "82-3-23". Bab. Library text.
K 22008 Library text.
K 22009 Ritual?
K 22010 Administrative?
K 22011 Library text.
K 22012 Religious?
K 22013 Late Babylonian administrative.
K 22014 Medical.
K 22015 Bab. Letter?
K 22016 Uncertain.
K 22017 Uncertain.
K 22018 "82-3-23". Neo-Assyrian letter?
K 22019 Omens.
K 22020 Lexical? Cf. Antagal Fragment g (Sm 1711: *MSL* XVII 250).
K 22021 Bab. Ritual?
K 22022 Uncertain.
K 22023 Astrology?
K 22024 Royal inscription of Tiglath-pileser I, *AKA* p. 69 v 5-7.
K 22025 +K 9992, dup. K 4868+, 6916, 10380, incantation.
K 22026 "82-3-23". Bab. Omens?
K 22027 Commentary?
K 22028 Bab.
K 22029 (+)K 1619a+. Royal inscription of Tiglath-pileser I, *AKA* p. 36 i 72-75.
K 22030 Royal inscription of Sargon II, end of 1st, beginning of 2nd campaign, cf. Lie p. 6 23-24.
K 22031 Medical?
K 22032 Incantations.

K 22033 (+)Sm 758 (+)Sm 1288. Urra=ḫubullu XIV 116-122 (*MSL* VIII/2 16).
K 22034 Literary?
K 22035 Bab. Religious?
K 22036 Omens?
K 22037 Bab. (+)K 2893+, Gattung II (*ArOr* 21 379ff.).
K 22038 Bab.
K 22039 Uncertain.
K 22040 Omens.
K 22041 Bilingual incantation, dup. *STT* 198 1-2?
K 22042 Astrology?
K 22043 "82-3-23". Uncertain.
K 22044 "82-3-23". Omens?
K 22045 "82-3-23". Bab. Prayer?
K 22046 (+)K 1619a, royal inscription of Tiglath-pileser I, *AKA* p. 81 vi 25-29.
K 22047 Literary/religious?
K 22048 Uncertain.
K 22049 Omens?
K 22050 Omens?
K 22051 Neo-Assyrian letter.
K 22052 Ritual or letter?
K 22053 Omens?
K 22054 Religious?
K 22055 Library text.
K 22056 Medical or ritual?
K 22057 Bab. Astrological omens, cf. *ACh* Supp. 2 Ištar CXIX 42-44.
K 22058 God list.
K 22059 Uncertain.
K 22060 Uncertain.
K 22061 "82-3-23". Text with glosses.
K 22062 Library text.
K 22063 Library text.
K 22064 Library text.
K 22065 Neo-Assyrian letter naming Marduk-apla-iddina.
K 22066 Uncertain.
K 22067 Bab. Uncertain.
K 22068 Omens?
K 22069 Literary?
K 22070 Library text.
K 22071 Uncertain.
K 22072 Bab. Bilingual?
K 22073 Bab. Bilingual.
K 22074 Bab. Uncertain.
K 22075 Library text.
K 22076 +K 14103, Urra=ḫubullu IV 53-58 (*MSL* V 154).
K 22077 Library text.
K 22078 Uncertain.
K 22079 Uncertain.
K 22080 Uncertain.
K 22081 Literary/religious.
K 22082 Library text.
K 22083 +BM 128018 (Th 1929-10-12, 674), Šurpu II 111-120.
K 22084 Bab. Library text.
K 22085 Library text.
K 22086 Library text.
K 22087 Middle Assyrian royal inscription?
K 22088 Library text.
K 22089 Medical ritual.
K 22090 Middle Assyrian royal inscription?
K 22091 Concerns eclipses.
K 22092 "82-3-23". Library text.
K 22093 +K 8524+, Enūma eliš I 136-140.
K 22094 "82-3-23". Late Babylonian administrative; from Sippar?
K 22095 Bab. Letter or omens?
K 22096 Library text.
K 22097 Bab. Library text.
K 22098 Bab. Omens.
K 22099 Bab. Library text.
K 22100 "82-3-23". Library text.
K 22101 Uncertain.
K 22102 "82-3-23". Bab. Library text.
K 22103 Library text.
K 22104 Library text.
K 22105 Uncertain.
K 22106 Literary?

K 22107 Commentary.
K 22108 Literary.
K 22109 Ashurbanipal prism fragment, dup. *VAB* VII p. 28 55-59.
K 22110 +K 22113. Ashurbanipal prism fragment, dup. *VAB* VII pp. 102-104 1-5.
K 22111 Ashurbanipal prism fragment, dup. *VAB* VII p. 2 6-9.
K 22112 Neo-Assyrian colophon.
K 22113 See K 22110.
K 22114 Uncertain.
K 22115 Uncertain.
K 22116 Uncertain.
K 22117 Lexical.
K 22118 Bab. Library text.
K 22119 Literary/religious?
K 22120 Plant list.
K 22121 Bab. Omens(?) and colophon.
K 22122 Library text.
K 22123 Library text.
K 22124 Omens.
K 22125 Literary?
K 22126 Astrological omens, dup. *ACh* Sin XXXV 45-49 = Enūma Anu Enlil XXII.
K 22127 Letter.
K 22128 "K". +K 2987b+ iii (Wiggerman, *BPF* p. 28) 164-168, ritual. See K 22178.
K 22129 Uncertain.
K 22130 Omens?
K 22131 "82-3-23". Uncertain.
K 22132 Library text.
K 22133 Omens or ritual?
K 22134 Uncertain.
K 22135 Neo-Assyrian legal document (witnesses).
K 22136 Bab. Administrative?
K 22137 Uncertain.
K 22138 Royal inscription of Ashurbanipal?
K 22139 Lexical. Nabnītu XIII 96-101 (*MSL* XVI 128)?
K 22140 Bab. Astrological omens, cf. *ACh* Adad XIX and *ACh* Supp. 2 XCIVb.
K 22141 Neo-Assyrian letter.
K 22142 Omens.
K 22143 Bab. Uncertain.
K 22144 Uncertain.
K 22145 Incantation?
K 22146 Ritual?
K 22147 Omens?
K 22148 Omens.
K 22149 Emesal.
K 22150 Astrological omens, Enūma Anu Enlil XXXV, dup. *ACh* Shamash XI 76-79, K 6719, K 8364.
K 22151 Medical ritual.
K 22152 Religious?
K 22153 +K 4465+, Gilgameš I 242-248.
K 22154 Mentions Enlil.
K 22155 Bab. Bilingual?
K 22156 +K 9936, Urra=ḫubullu XV gap C(?) and 299 (*MSL* IX 3ff.).
K 22157 Middle Assyrian royal inscription?
K 22158 Bab. Administration?
K 22159 Literary/religious?
K 22160 Neo-Assyrian ritual?
K 22161 (+)K 1620a. Royal inscription of Tiglath-pileser I, *AKA* p. 63 iv 44-48.
K 22162 (+)K 1620a. Royal inscription of Tiglath-pileser I, *AKA* p. 62 iv 32-35.
K 22163 Lexical, Ana ittišu VI ii 55-57 (*MSL* I 82).
K 22164 Incantations.
K 22165 Literary/religious.
K 22166 Omens or litany?
K 22167 Prayer.
K 22168 Literary/religious?
K 22169 End of text and colophon?
K 22170 Medical.
K 22171 Bab. Literary/religious.

K 22172 Religious.
K 22173 Bab. Literary/religious.
K 22174 Ritual or incantation?
K 22175 Omens?
K 22176 Ritual.
K 22177 Astrological omens, to *ACh* Ištar XXIII.
K 22178 Ritual, (+)K 2987b? See K 22128.
K 22179 Bilingual?
K 22180 Bilingual religious.
K 22181 Uncertain.
K 22182 Omens.
K 22183 Literary or list of cereals?
K 22184 *Sikkatu* fragment, dup. *AAA* 19 103 4 (Sargon II).
K 22185 *Sikkatu* fragment.
K 22186 *Sikkatu* fragment.
K 22187 *Sikkatu* fragment.
K 22188 *Sikkatu* fragment.
K 22189 *Sikkatu* fragment.
K 22190 *Sikkatu* fragment.
K 22191 *Sikkatu* fragment.
K 22192 *Sikkatu* fragment, dup. *AAA* 19 103 6 (Sargon II).
K 22193 *Sikkatu* fragment.
K 22194 Bilingual incantation.
K 22195 *Sikkatu* fragment.
K 22196 *Sikkatu* fragment.
K 22197 *Sikkatu* fragment.
K 22198 *Sikkatu* fragment.
K 22199 *Sikkatu* fragment.
K 22200 *Sikkatu* fragment.
K 22201 *Sikkatu* fragment?
K 22202 *Sikkatu* fragment.

APPENDIX

This appendix lists Assyrian texts in the BM collections not included in the Kouyunjik catalogues. Unless stated otherwise all items listed are Neo-Assyrian tablets and presumed to come from Assyria. The list includes other items which have for various reasons entered the Kouyunjik Collection, and the Neo-Assyrian royal inscriptions from Babylonia in Babylonian script.

This list does not include tablets deriving from the excavations at Nimrud conducted by the British School of Archaeology in Iraq under the direction of M. E. L. Mallowan in 1949-63, nor tablets deriving from the German excavations at Tell Halaf in 1911-13 (BM 114900-115011 = 1920-12-11, 228-339), which are fully accounted for in J. Friedrich et al., *Die Inschriften vom Tell Halaf* (*AfO* Beiheft 6).

The Th. 1905-4-9, 1929-10-12, 1930-5-8, 1932-12-10, and 1932-12-12 collections come from the British Museum's excavations at Nineveh. For an explanation of Nineveh find-spots see W. G. Lambert and A. R. Millard, *Catalogue of the Cuneiform Tablets in the Kouyunjik Collection of the British Museum:*, *Second Supplement*, p. xi. The 1911-4-8 collection comes from the German excavations at Ashur. The 1953-10-10 collection was transferred to the BM from the Brighton and Hove Museum, having been presented to that museum by Hormuzd Rassam. The 1955-4-16 collection was presented by the Margate Public Libraries.

Readers should also note the supplementary list of tablets published in the fourth volume of this Catalogue, p. xii.

BM	Registration	
-	Sm 2248	*Sikkatu* fragment.
-	48-7-20, 120	Bab.; +48-7-20, 117 (*ABL* 1089), letter; Layard, *ICC* pl. 30.
-	80-7-19, 261	Uncertain.
-	82-8-16, 1	Lexical; Diri IV; *CT* 11, 49-50.
25026	98-2-16, 80	Royal inscription of Ashurbanipal; prism, dup. *VAB* VII 46 v 41-54, 50 vi 7-29.
28384	98-10-11, 20	+BM 50843. Bab. Royal inscription of Ashurbanipal; cylinder; dup. *VAB* VII pp. 228-232.
30011	-	Omens or medical; probably acquired between 1848 and 1870.
30153	-	Bab. Royal inscription of Esarhaddon; prism; M. Cogan, *AfO* 31, 75.
30211	48-11-4, 318	Middle Assyrian script; troops assigned to city gates; *līmu* Mušallim-Adad; A. R. George, *Iraq* 50 31ff.
32646	76-11-17, 2413	Royal inscription of Ashurbanipal(?); prism.

32647	76-11-17, 2414	Lexical; Urra = ḫubullu XI 241-307 (*MSL* VII 138-140) or Uruanna III (Köcher, *Pflanzen* no. 23)?
32648	76-11-17, 2415	Lexical, Malku VI.
32649	76-11-17, 2416	Royal inscription of Ashurbanipal, dup. *VAB* VII 52 vi 36-43.
32650	76-11-17, 2417	Liver omens.
36711	80-6-17, 443	Neo-Assyrian; list of officials.
40074		Royal inscription of Ashurbanipal; cylinder fragment, dup. *VAB* VII 226-228 7-21.
42668	81-7-1,430	Royal inscription of Esarhaddon; prism; *AfO* 24 118 and pl. XIII.
45793	81-7-6, 210	Bab. Royal inscription of Esarhaddon; cylinder; *BA* 3 351-353 (as 81-6-7, 209); Borger, *Asarhaddon* pp. 73-75 "Uruk A"; previously numbered BM 12173 and 91031.
47655	81-11-3,360	(+)BM 47656. Royal inscription of Ashurbanipal; cylinder fragment; dup. *VAB* VII 234-238 1-4, 24-29.
47656	81-11-3,361	(+)BM 47655, which see.
49222	82-3-23, 213	Unidentified.
50582	82-3-23, 1573	Bab. Royal inscription of Esarhaddon? Dup. BM 56628; cf. BM 56617.
50662	82-3-23, 1653	Bab. Royal inscription of Ashurbanipal; cylinder; dup. *VAB* VII pp. 234-236 1-10.
50768-82	82-3-23, 1760-74	Bullae; all with stamp seal impressions, a few with writing.
50790-99	82-3-23, 1782-91	Bullae, with stamp seal impressions.
50843	82-3-23, 1837	+BM 28384, which see.
-	82-3-23, 5146	Bulla, with stamp seal impressions.
-	82-3-23, 5148-59	Bullae, with stamp seal impressions.
-	82-3-23, 5185	Bulla, with stamp seal impressions.
50999	82-3-23, 1995	Lexical; list of garments?
56617	82-7-14, 996b+1815	Bab. Royal inscription of Esarhaddon; prism.
56628	82-7-14, 1010	Bab. Royal inscription of Esarhaddon? Dup. BM 50582; cf. BM 56617.
56634	82-7-14, 1032	Bab. Royal inscription of Ashurbanipal; cylinder; dup. BM 91115. Archaizing script.
56639	82-7-14, 1044	Bab. Royal inscription of Ashurbanipal; cylinder; dup. BM 91115.
60032	82-7-14, 4442	Bab. Royal inscription of Esarhaddon; prism; *AfO* 24, 117.
62231	82-9-18, 2200	Prayer.
65217	82-9-18, 5200	+BM 66616 (82-9-18, 6609); *Iraq* 46, 69; musical.
66616	82-9-18, 6609	+BM 65217, which see.

68368	82-9-18, 8366	+80-7-19, 193; lexical, Urra = ḫubullu X, see *MSL* VII 71.
68613	82-9-18, 8612	Bab. Royal inscription of Ashurbanipal; cylinder; dup. *CT* 9, 6-7; cf. *VAB* VII p. 234f.
69427	82-9-18, 9424	Prayer and ritual.
69428	82-9-18, 9425	Neo-Babylonian (from Nineveh?).
73164	82-9-18, 13175	Neo-Assyrian, legal; stamp-seal impressions; Kalḫu, 14/-/ *līmu* Šamaš-kāšid-ayyābi (=669 BC).
76091	AH 83-1-18, 1456	Neo-Assyrian legal.
77023	AH 83-1-18, 2398	Inscribed bulla.
78179	Bu. 88-5-12, 11	Hemerology; *CT* 4, 5-6.
78221	Bu. 88-5-12, 74	+BM 78222. Bab. Royal inscription of Esarhaddon, prism, *CT* 44 5-7 no. 5.
78222	Bu. 88-5-12, 75+76	+BM 78221, which see.
78223	Bu. 88-5-12, 77+78	Bab. Royal inscription of Esarhaddon, prism, *CT* 44 2-3 no. 3.
78224	Bu. 88-5-12, 79	+BM 132294. Bab. Royal inscription of Esarhaddon, prism, *CT* 44 4 no. 4 and *AfO* 24 117.
78225	Bu. 88-5-12, 80	Bab. Royal inscription of Esarhaddon, prism, *CT* 44 8 no. 6.
78246	Bu. 88-5-12, 101	Bab. Royal inscription of Esarhaddon, prism, *CT* 44 8 no. 8.
78247	Bu. 88-5-12, 102	Royal inscription of Esarhaddon, prism, *CT* 44 9 no. 9.
78248	Bu. 88-5-12, 103	Bab. Royal inscription of Esarhaddon, prism, *CT* 44 9 no. 7.
78264	Bu. 88-5-12, 120	Bab. Royal inscription of Ashurbanipal, cylinder, dup.*VAB* VII pp. 228-233.
78432	Bu. 88-5-12, 335	Prayer to Sîn; S. H. Langdon, *PSBA* 40, 104-110, *UFBG* p. 408.
78955	Bu. 89-4-26, 250	Incantations and rituals against fear and nightmares.
78960	Bu. 89-4-26, 255	Šumma ālu; snake omens.
79035	Bu. 89-4-26, 332	Neo-Assyrian oracle question (cf. *SAA* IV).
79037	Bu. 89-4-26, 334	Middle Assyrian script; Sumerian litany with Akkadian glosses.
79099	Bu. 89-4-26, 396	Neo-Assyrian letter.
79106	Bu. 89-4-26, 403	+ K 7815+. Medical.
79454	Bu. 89-4-26, 751	Royal inscription of Ashurbanipal (?).
79503	89-10-14, 51	Copy of a bilingual votive inscription of Adad-apla-iddina with colophon of the time of Esarhaddon; *StOr* 1, 22-33.
83001	83-1-21, 164	Royal inscription of Ashurbanipal, cylinder fragment, dup.*VAB* VII 238 19-30.
88347	1901-2-9, 64	Middle Assyrian script; *sikkatu*.

90817	1979-12-20, 366	Assyrian royal inscription, 10th-9th century B.C.; inscribed with a red number 298 similar to those found on DT tablets.
91107	82-7-14, 1000	Bab. Royal inscription of Šamaš-šuma-ukîn; barrel cylinder; Lehmann, *Šamaššumukîn*, pt. 3, p. 12-13, pl. 8.
91115	82-7-14, 1043	Bab. Royal inscription of Ashurbanipal; cylinder; V *R* 62, 1; *VAB* VII 228f.
93088	82-5-22, 300a	Royal inscription of Sennacherib; vessel; *Iraq* 42, 84f.
93014	82-5-22, 1048	+ 82-3-23, 101; bilingual incantations; *CT* 13, 35-38; Bab.; registered as coming from Kouyunjik.
98940	Th. 1905-4-9, 446	(+)K 1698. Royal inscription of Ashurbanipal; prism, dup. *VAB* VII 44ff. v 16-38, vi 21-28.
98941	Th. 1905-4-9, 447	Middle Assyrian; historical epic ; *CT* 34, 15-16.
98942	Th. 1905-4-9, 448	Medical.
103016	1909-5-11, 1	Letter; *CT* 53 no 974.
103017	1909-5-11, 2	Loan contract; *ZA* 73 238-239, 250 no. 7; *SAAB* III/2 69-74.
103187	1910-10-8, 115	Incantation prayer.
103200	1910-10-8, 128	Middle Assyrian script; administrative, *līmu* Ibri-šarri.
103202	1910-10-8, 130	Loan contract; *ZA* 73 239-240, 251 no. 8.
103204	1910-10-8, 132	Neo-Assyrian administrative.
103205	1910-10-8, 133	Memorandum on ŠIM Išḫara; *ZA* 73 245-246, 252 no. 12.
103206	1910-10-8, 134	Lawsuit; *līmu* Aššur-ilāya (653 BC); *ZA* 73 241-242, 252 no. 9.
103207	1910-10-8, 135	Middle Assyrian script; administrative.
103385	1911-4-8, 75	Incantations; ka-inim-ma é-gal-ku$_4$-ra; joins VAT 13651 (*LKA* 107) and A 3445.
103386	1911-4-8, 76	Medical
103387	1911-4-8, 77	Royal decree of Adad-nīrāri III concerning offerings for the temple of Ashur at Ashur; *CT* 33, 13-14; joins VAT 8920+9633+9634 (E. F. Weidner, *AfO* 21, 36f.) and Kelsey 89518 ; Postgate, *NRGD* no 42.
103388	1911-4-8, 78	*Sikkatu* fragment; *CT* 32, 9; Grayson, *ARI* 1, 45 no 5; *RIMA* 1 73.2.2.
103389	1911-4-8, 79	Sale contract; *ZA* 73 242-243, 253 no. 10; *AfO* 32 38-42.
103390	1911-4-8, 80	Neo-Assyrian letter; F. M. Fales, *ZA* 73, 246-249, 253 no 13; K. Deller, *Or.Ant.* 25, 21-27.
103391	1911-4-8, 81	Neo-Assyrian legal; *CT* 33, 18.
103391a	1911-4-8, 81a	Envelope of preceding; *CT* 33, 18.
103392	1911-4-8, 82	Neo-Assyrian legal; *CT* 33, 19.
103392a	1911-4-8, 82a	Envelope of preceding; *CT* 33, 19.

103393	1911-4-8, 83	Neo-Assyrian legal; *CT* 33, 17; K. Deller, *JESHO* 30, 19-29.
103393a	1911-4-8, 83a	Envelope of preceding; *CT* 33, 17; K. Deller, *JESHO* 30, 19-29.
103394	1911-4-8, 84	Neo-Assyrian legal; *CT* 33, 16.
103394a	1911-4-8, 84a	Envelope of preceding; *CT* 33, 16.
103395	1911-4-8, 85	Amulet-shaped tablet; administrative; *CT* 33, 15.
103396	1911-4-8, 86	Neo-Assyrian legal; *CT* 33, 15.
103956	1911-4-8, 646	Sale contract; *ZA* 73 243-245, 250 no. 11.
104727	1912-5-13, 2	+Sm 2116. Historical epic naming Adad-šuma-uṣur and Enlil-kudurra-uṣur.
105315	1913-4-16, 147	See BM 117901 and 117903-117906.
108775	1914-2-14, 1	Royal inscription of Sargon II; 9-sided prism; D. G.Lyon, *AB* 5, 1-12 (as L.2). From Khorsabad; bequeathed by H. F. B. Lynch.
108859	1914-4-7, 25	Lexical, plant list; *CT* 37, 26-28, dup. Köcher, *Pflanzen* no. 28.
108860	1914-4-7, 26	Lexical, plant list, Uruanna(?); *CT* 37, 28-32.
108861	1914-4-7, 27	Lexical, list of professional titles, Urra = ḫubullu XXV (?); *CT* 37, 24-25; *MSL* XII 227-230.
108862	1914-4-7, 28	Middle Assyrian script; lexical; Ea I; *CT* 35, 1-8 = *MSL* XIV, 173.
108872	1914-4-7, 38	(+)BM 109097a; medical.
109097a	1914-4-7, 147	(+)BM 108872; medical.
113203	1915-4-10, 1	Royal inscription of Sennacherib; S. Smith, *The First Campaign of Sennacherib*.
114835	1920-12-13, 127	Neo-Assyrian court decision.
114836	1920-12-13, 128	Neo-Assyrian letter, mentions Qu'e.
115635	DT 382	Clay fist with inscription of Ashurnaṣirpal II.
116229	1922-5-11,362	Unidentified.
116230	1922-5-11, 363	Legal; Woolley, *Carchemish* II 135-142 and pl. 26a; Postgate, *Taxation*, 360f.
116358	N.1986	Inscribed tablet covered with a layer of clay; from Kouyunjik or Nimrud? A. H. Layard's excavations.
117901	1926-2-15, 21	+BM 105315+ (1913-4-16,147+); royal inscription of Ashurbanipal; prism.
117902	1926-2-15, 22	+BM 127836; royal inscription of Ashurbanipal; prism, dup. *VAB* VII 1ff.
117903	1926-2-15, 23	+BM 105315 (1913-4-16,147+); see BM 117901.
117904	1926-2-15, 24	+BM 105315 (1913-4-16,147+); see BM 117901.
117905	1926-2-15, 25	+BM 105315 (1913-4-16,147+); see BM 117901.
117906	1926-2-15, 26	+BM 105315 (1913-4-16,147+); see BM 117901.
120066	1928-7-16, 66	+Ki.1902-5-10, 6; royal inscription of Esarhaddon; cylinder; *AfO* 31 73.

120116	1928-2-11, 96	Middle Assyrian script; *sikkatu*; Shalmaneser I; Grayson, *ARI* 1, 85 no 2 = *IAK* 126 no 2: 13-25; *RIMA* 1 77.2.14.
120122	1928-2-11, 102	Middle Assyrian script; horse-training text (cf. Ebeling, *BVW*).
121206	1930-5-12, 1	Neo-Assyrian cultic; G. van Driel, *The Cult of Ashur* (cf. *Or* 40, 90-1).
122698	1931-4-17, 1	Neo-Assyrian legal; division of an inheritance; from Ashur; *AfO* 32 42-52.
130660	1948-11-13, 1	Middle Assyrian script; bilingual incantations; Udugḫul XII; M. J. Geller, *Iraq* 42, 23-4; presented by C. Clough.
131653	1953-10-10, 1	Omens.
131654	1953-10-10, 2	+K 2275+; astrological omens.
131655	1953-10-10, 3	Omens.
131656	1953-10-10, 4	Šumma ālu LXXXIV; E. F.Weidner, *AfO* 11, 359 and pl. 1; from Kalḫu.
131657	1953-10-10, 5	Liver omens.
131658	1953-10-10, 6	Liver omens.
132019	1955-4-16, 1	Lexical and literary extracts; Urra=ḫubullu VI 191-193, etc.
132020	1955-4-16, 2	Lexical and literary extracts; Urra=ḫubullu XIVff., etc.
132021	1955-4-16, 3	Lexical and literary extracts; Urgud A II 250-252, Igituḫ I 103-105, Fire incantation, *AfO* 23 41 20-21, etc.
132227	1957-10-16, 1	Medical.
132294	1958-4-12, 28	+BM 78224, which see.
132980	1962-7-23, 1	Letter.
134608	1932-12-12, 603	Royal inscription of Ashurbanipal; prism fragment; cf.*VAB* VII 218-220 2-15.
134609	1932-12-12, 604	Royal inscription of Ashurbanipal; prism fragment; concerning Ḫallusi.
134610	1932-12-12, 605	Royal inscription of Sennacherib; prism fragment; cf. *OIP* II 99-100.
135586	1971-7-5, 1	Neo-Assyrian letter; S. Parpola, *Iraq* 34, 21-34.
135909	1973-6-18, 1	Gilgamesh XII; E. F. Weidner, *AfO* 10, 363-365; presented by D. Opitz.
135910	1973-7-21, 1	Middle Assyrian script; historical; A. K. Grayson, *Iraq* 37, 71-74; presented by H. E. L. Mellersh.
137310	1932-12-12, 907	Old Babylonian; *līmu* Adad-bāni; Nineveh, WW6.
137311	1932-12-12, 908	Bilingual; Nineveh, MM-5.
138182	1932-12-12, 909	+BM 138194; royal inscription of Ashurbanipal; prism; M. Cogan, *JCS* 35, 146.
138183	1932-12-12, 910	Royal inscription of Ashurbanipal; prism; M. Cogan, *JCS* 35, 146.

138184	1932-12-12, 911	Royal inscription of Esarhaddon; prism, Nin. A; M. Cogan, *AfO* 31, 72.
138185	1932-12-12, 912	Royal inscription of Sennacherib; prism, dup. *OIP* II 25 41-59, 29 21-32.
138186	1932-12-12, 913	Royal inscription of Ashurbanipal; prism, dup. *VAB* VII 4 11-21, 86 68-75.
138187	1932-12-12, 914	Royal inscription of Ashurbanipal; prism; M. Cogan, *JCS* 35, 146.
138188	1932-12-12, 915	+BM 127837+; royal inscription of Sennacherib; prism.
138189	1932-12-12, 916	Royal inscription of Ashurbanipal; prism; M. Cogan, *JCS* 32, 150.
138190	1932-12-12, 917	Neo-Assyrian royal inscription; prism.
138191	1932-12-12, 918	+BM 138193; royal inscription of Ashurbanipal; prism; (+)BM 127873?, see M. Cogan *JCS* 32, 150.
138192	1932-12-12, 919	+BM 127909+; royal inscription of Ashurbanipal; prism; M. Cogan, *JCS* 32, 147-9.
138193	1932-12-12, 920	+BM 138191, which see.
138194	1932-12-12, 921	+BM 138182, which see.
138195	1980-7-28, 1	+BM 127872+; royal inscription of Esarhaddon; prism; *līmu* Atar-ili of Laḫiru; M. Cogan, *AfO* 31,72.
138580	1932-12-12, 1113	Fragment of an archaic tablet with seal impressions and numbers (Uruk period); Nineveh, NV; D. Collon and J. E. Reade, *Baghdader Mitteilungen* 14 33-34.
138581	1932-12-12, 1114	Fragment of an archaic tablet with seal impressions; Nineveh, MM-12; D. Collon and J. E. Reade, *Baghdader Mitteilungen* 14 38-39.
138659	1932-12-12, 1192	Edge of tablet; traces; Nineveh, MM-54.
138720	1932-12-12, 1253	Inscribed clay fist; Nineveh, MM3.
138726	1932-12-12, 1259	Inscribed piece of storage vessel.
139229	1929-10-12, 875	*Sikkatu* fragments, the majority with inscription, many of
-139245	-891	Ashurnāṣirpal II.
139246	1932-12-10, 700	*Sikkatu* fragments, the majority with inscription, many of
-139320	-774	Ashurnāṣirpal II.
139321	1930-5-8, 234	*Sikkatu* fragments, the majority with inscription, many of
-139341	-254	Ashurnāṣirpal II. BM 139325 joins BM 123530 (1932-12-10, 473).
139342	1930-5-8, 255	Fragment of vessel with cuneiform sign. CHOL.
139343	1930-5-8, 256	Neo-Assyrian prism fragment. CHOL. SH. 84.
139344	1930-5-8, 257	Neo-Assyrian tablet with colophon. 1930. 13.
139345	1930-5-8, 258	Neo-Assyrian tablet, illegible.
139346	1930-5-8, 259	Library tablet. TEL. 88.

139347	1930-5-8, 260	Library tablet.
139348	1930-5-8, 261	Middle Assyrian tablet, royal inscription. CHOL. 1930. 106.
139349	1930-5-8, 262	No script.
139355a	1932-12-10, 777a	Neo-Assyrian royal inscription; prism fragment.
139355b	1932-12-10, 777b	Neo-Assyrian royal inscription; prism fragment.
139355c	1932-12-10, 777c	Neo-Assyrian royal inscription; prism fragment.
139436	1983-1-1, 11	Cast of a fragment of omens from eclipses.
139508	1983-1-1, 51	Royal inscription; prism fragment.
139525	1984-1-21, 1	Administrative; barley-docket; stamp seal impressions.
139950	1985-7-14, 1	Legal, land rental, mentions Bīt-abī-ilāya, dated 18/v *līmu* Aššur-māta-taqqin; stamp-seal impressions and Aramaic note.
139971	1985-10-6, 8	Neo-Assyrian royal dedication; formerly numbered 1903.4 in the collection of Lord Amherst of Hackney.
141624	1990-12-15, 1	Middle Assyrian script; administrative; provisions for the king; *līmu* Bēr-išmânni.
141627	1991-1-27, 1	Economic, concerning goods and silver, mentioning the governor of Harran.

INDEX

Unless otherwise indicated all numbers within the range 16801-22202 are K (Kouyunjik) numbers.

17508 (Gula Hymn of Bulluṭsa-rabi), 17592, 17600 (bilingual), 17617 (Sumerian), 17762, 17795, 17804, 17828, 17941, 17958, 18092, 18103 (to Adad), 18129 (to Šarrat Nippuri), 18164, 18242, 18699 (Bab.), 18931, 19044 (Bab.), 19052 (Bab., to Eru'a), 19215, 19570, 19574 (bilingual, to Ashur?), 19629, 19656, 19657 (to Ningirsu?), 19671 (to Ištar), 19789 (bilingual, to Nanay), 19886, 19932 (to a goddess), 20055, 20077, 20178, 20290, 20637 (Šamaš Hymn), 20709, 20806, 20869, 21073, 21127 (Bab.), 21145 (bilingual), 21422, 21889 (to Šarrat Nippuri), 21958

Ikrib's: 16802, 17114, 17816 (Bab.), 17846, 17976, 19348 (Bab.), 19768
images: 18835, 19482, 19557
Inanna: 19826
incantations: 16824, 16826 (bilingual, Udugḫul), 16912, 16918 (ki.^{d}utu.kam; Bīt rimki?), 16958 (bilingual), 17033 (bilingual), 17078, 17111, 17143 (Sumerian), 17149 (bilingual or Akkadian), 17151 (bilingual), 17158 (bilingual), 17202 (bilingual; Bīt rimki), 17223, 17225, 17344 (toothache), 17541 (bilingual), 17546, 17550 (Sumerian), 17627 (bilingual; Mīs pî?), 17678, 17680 (bilingual), 17707 (Sumerian), 17712 (Sumerian), 17737 (bilingual), 17766 (fire incantation), 17782 (bilingual), 17808 (fire incantations), 17869, 17907 (Sumerian), 17922 (incantation prayer to Marduk), 17984 (Maqlû-type), 18115 (Šimmatu), 18211 (bilingual; Šurpu), 18364 (incantation prayer), 18419, 18422, 18448 (Sumerian), 18539, 18618 (Maqlû-type), 18673, 18819, 18917 (bilingual; Marduk-Ea type), 18992 (Bab.), 19044 (Bab.), 19066 (incantation prayer), 19154 (Bab.) (Maqlû-type), 19178, 19267, 19379 (bilingual), 19449 (Lamaštu), 19455 (incantation prayer), 19475 (Akkadian; Lamaštu), 19590 (Sumerian), 19594, 19598 (bilingual; Marduk-Ea type), 19623 (bilingual), 19675, 19704, 19705, 19714, 19752 (bilingual), 19796 (bilingual), 19806, 19870, 19882 (bilingual), 19920, 19926 (bilingual), 19995 (bilingual), 20030, 20043 (Maqlû-type), 20073, 20135 (Bab.), 20139, 20159, 20163, 20166, 20269 (bilingual), 20274 (Bab., bilingual), 20278, 20283, 20363 (bilingual exorcistic), 20382 (bilingual; Udugḫul?), 20383 (bilingual), 20384 (bilingual), 20447 (Sumerian), 20533 (Sumerian; Mīs pî?), 20547 (Sumerian), 20554 (bilingual), 20555 (bilingual; Šurpu), 20638 (bilingual), 20669 (bilingual), 20687, 20701, 20721 (Sagalla), 20776 (Sumerian), 20922 (bilingual), 20960 (bilingual), 20969, 20975 (bilingual), 21029, 21032 (bilingual), 21071 (dream incantations), 21094 (Sumerian), 21120, 21161 (bilingual), 21230, 21236 (bilingual), 21243, 21388 (bilingual), 21400 (Sumerian), 21431, 21432 (bilingual), 21653 (Bab., incantation prayer to Marduk), 21689 (Bab.), 21847 (bilingual; Mīs pî?), 21855 (bilingual), 21993, 22025, 22032, 22041 (bilingual), 22145, 22164, 22174, 22194 (bilingual), BM 78955 (against nightmares), 93014 (bilingual), 103187 (prayer), 103385, 130660 (Middle Assyrian; bilingual, Udugḫul 12), 132021 (Fire incantation).
Iqqur īpuš: 17213, 17785 (colophon), 18713, 19061 (Bab.)
Isin II inscriptions: 17301, 18603, 21096
Išḫara: BM 103205
Ištar: 17081, 17519, 17982, 18564, 19577, 19671, 21418 (of Nineveh)

jewelry: 19195

Kalḫu: BM 73164
Kulaba: 20668
Kulla: 17940
Kusu: 17824

Lamaštu: 17781, 18615, 19449, 19475
laments: 16910 (bilingual), 17372 (bilingual), 17696 (Sumerian), 19826 (bilingual, Inanna of Uruk)
legal: 16861 (conveyance), 17169, 17799, 17921 (conveyance), 17997, 18375 (witness list), 19211, 19288 (conveyance), 19433, 19478, 19599 (conveyance), 19693 (Late Babylonian), 19824, 19424, 20190

Šumma ālu: 16805 (colophon), 16892, 17032, 17431, 17439, 17511, 17635, 17871, 18020, 18236,18888 (Bab.), 19326, 20060, 20157, 20342, 20455 (colophon), 20465 (colophon), 20600, 21017, 21021, 21702 (mentioned in a letter), 21705 (reeds), 21854 (incipits?), 21894, 21946, BM 78960, 131656
Šumma izbu: 17822, 19224 (Bab.), 19305, 19755 (commentary), 21954
tongue: 20124
unidentified: 16816, 16820, 16829, 16830, 16835, 16837, 16839, 16844, 16846, 16851, 16856, 16857, 16858, 16863, 16868, 16870, 16871, 16874, 16884, 16890, 16893, 16904, 16906, 16913, 16914, 16916, 16936, 16946, 16951, 16952, 16964, 16966, 16967, 16970, 16973, 16974, 16975, 16981, 16985, 16991, 16999, 17007, 17015, 17017, 17020, 17027, 17029, 17035, 17038, 17039, 17044, 17049, 17050, 17052, 17060, 17068, 17073, 17076, 17077 (Bab.), 17080, 17083, 17103, 17106, 17112, 17116, 17118, 17152, 17153, 17156, 17160, 17163, 17167, 17170, 17172, 17182, 17184, 17188, 17189, 17190, 17191, 17192, 17203 (Bab.), 17209, 17217, 17218, 17219, 17224, 17228, 17229, 17230, 17234, 17236, 17243, 17245, 17248, 17253, 17256, 17261, 17264, 17267, 17268, 17270, 17272, 17276, 17277, 17278, 17288, 17289 (Bab.), 17297, 17298, 17299, 17302, 17304, 17308, 17311, 17314, 17319, 17323, 17324, 17327, 17332, 17334, 17336, 17337, 17338, 17340, 17341, 17345, 17348, 17350, 17351, 17355, 17357, 17363, 17364, 17375 (Bab.), 17378, 17382, 17384, 17387, 17393, 17396, 17399, 17414, 17419, 17432, 17435, 17438, 17440, 17442, 17444, 17449, 17450, 17459, 17461, 17464, 17465, 17466, 17473, 17476, 17483, 17488, 17494, 17496, 17500, 17505, 17512, 17513, 17518, 17542, 17543, 17553, 17554, 17556, 17557, 17559, 17563, 17564, 17565, 17567, 17568, 17572, 17575, 17577, 17587, 17594, 17597, 17599, 17602, 17603, 17604, 17606, 17609, 17619, 17620, 17625, 17626, 17636 (Bab.), 17637, 17643, 17645, 17654 (Bab.), 17659, 17662, 17663, 17672, 17673, 17676, 17684, 17686, 17689, 17691, 17698, 17701, 17702, 17713, 17716, 17719, 17720, 17721, 17727, 17728, 17732, 17733, 17734, 17746, 17747, 17751, 17757, 17759, 17764, 17772, 17777, 17784, 17793, 17806, 17811, 17847, 17860, 17864, 17865, 17866, 17867, 17868, 17873, 17877, 17878, 17881, 17884, 17886, 17888, 17893, 17895, 17899, 17903, 17904, 17910, 17915, 17916, 17917, 17919, 17920, 17924, 17925, 17926, 17929, 17930, 17933, 17944, 17960, 17961, 17967, 17969, 17975, 17981, 17998, 18002, 18004, 18011, 18014, 18015, 18016, 18024, 18025, 18034, 18066, 18067, 18069, 18070, 18073, 18074, 18085, 18086 (Bab.), 18088, 18090, 18112, 18148, 18149, 18150, 18155, 18156, 18159, 18165, 18171, 18181, 18182, 18207, 18212, 18227, 18231, 18233, 18238, 18244, 18246, 18249, 18252, 18256, 18279, 18281, 18284, 18292, 18293, 18300, 18301, 18314, 18324, 18333, 18336, 18349, 18350, 18355, 18361, 18366, 18369, 18372, 18385, 18387, 18388, 18389, 18409, 18410, 18420, 18426, 18433, 18442, 18446, 18458, 18462, 18464, 18465, 18466, 18468, 18484, 18496, 18497, 18517, 18532, 18540, 18555, 18557, 18559, 18560, 18562, 18566, 18569, 18581, 18582, 18590 (Bab.), 18593 (Bab.), 18596, 18606, 18608 (Bab.), 18613 (Bab.), 18621, 18635, 18640, 18650, 18658 (Bab.), 18660 (Bab.), 18662, 18670, 18675, 18676 (Bab.), 18685, 18688 (Bab.), 18700, 18708 (Bab.), 18714, 18717, 18731 (Bab.), 18737, 18741, 18746, 18750 (Bab.), 18751 (Bab.), 18753 (Middle Assyrian), 18763, 18764 (Bab.), 18766 (Bab.), 18770 (Bab.), 18775 (Bab.), 18777 (Bab.), 18779 (Bab.), 18798, 18799, 18809, 18816 (*apālu*), 18824, 18825, 18831, 18832, 18838, 18840, 18841, 18849, 18852, 18857, 18859, 18865, 18868 (Bab.), 18879, 18882, 18883, 18885, 18902, 18910, 18913, 18915, 18916, 18921, 18926, 18934, 18936, 18937, 18938, 18944, 18953, 18961, 18962 (Bab.), 18964, 18966, 18970 (Bab.), 18978, 18984 (Bab.), 18987 (Bab.), 18989 (Bab.), 18990 (Bab.), 18993 (Bab.), 18995 (Bab.), 18999

(Bab.), 19002 (Bab.), 19006, 19010 (Bab.), 19017 (Bab.), 19022 (Bab.), 19026 (Bab.), 19028 (Bab.), 19040, 19042, 19045, 19054, 19058, 19063 (Bab.), 19070 (Bab.), 19072 (Bab.), 19075 (Bab.), 19078 (Bab.), 19079, 19084 (Bab.), 19085 (Bab.), 19086 (Bab.), 19088, 19091 (Bab.), 19099, 19100 (Bab.), 19102 (Bab.), 19107, 19109, 19114 (Bab.), 19120, 19121, 19130, 19135, 19136 (commentary?), 19137 (Bab.), 19138 (Bab.), 19142 (Bab.), 19143 (Sargon of Akkad), 19155, 19165, 19172, 19173, 19177, 19181, 19189 (Bab.), 19190 (Bab.), 19191, 19193 (Bab.), 19199, 19200 (Bab.), 19203, 19206, 19209 (Bab.), 19212 (Bab.), 19214 (Bab.), 19218 (Bab.), 19220, 19227 (Bab.), 19229, 19231, 19246, 19251, 19252, 19259, 19262, 19286, 19292, 19296 (Bab.), 19297 (Bab.), 19306, 19318, 19319 (Bab.), 19330 (Bab.), 19331 (Bab.), 19338, 19343 (Bab.), 19347 (Bab.), 19349 (Bab.), 19356 (Bab.), 19361 (Bab.), 19365 (Bab.), 19366, 19382, 19385, 19395, 19400, 19406, 19411, 19412 (Bab.), 19415, 19418, 19420, 19443, 19462, 19463, 19466, 19467, 19476, 19481, 19483, 19494, 19496 (Bab.), 19497, 19498, 19508, 19510, 19514, 19518, 19523, 19524, 19533, 19542, 19555 (first "*pirsu*"), 19566, 19578, 19595, 19602, 19611 (Bab.), 19654, 19666 (Bab.), 19672, 19685, 19697, 19700 (Bab.), 19702, 19708, 19710 (Bab.), 19716, 19720, 19728, 19729, 19738, 19739, 19747 (Bab.), 19763, 19773, 19783, 19791 (Bab.), 19792, 19799, 19801 (Bab.), 19804, 19810, 19812, 19819, 19823, 19829, 19842 (Bab.), 19843, 19844, 19845, 19849, 19853, 19856, 19862, 19866, 19869, 19875, 19877, 19887, 19904, 19921, 19925, 19929, 19934 (Bab.), 19936, 19944, 19960, 19970, 19981, 19984, 19993, 20001, 20005, 20016, 20018, 20021, 20022, 20023 (months), 20024, 20028, 20029, 20040, 20041, 20047, 20049, 20052, 20056, 20065, 20088, 20090, 20099, 20100, 20102, 20103, 20111, 20114, 20127, 20130, 20202, 20211, 20213, 20243, 20244, 20246, 20247, 20248, 20251, 20256, 20260, 20262 (Bab.), 20263, 20286, 20298, 20299 (Bab.), 20302, 20305, 20308, 20309, 20311, 20312, 20313 (Bab.), 20314, 20316, 20321, 20322, 20328, 20332 (Bab.), 20334, 20335, 20339, 20344, 20345, 20346, 20347, 20349, 20350, 20351, 20352, 20380, 20389, 20435, 20436, 20605, 20629, 20636, 20650, 20653, 20657, 20666, 20670, 20690 (Bab.), 20696, 20700, 20705, 20708, 20713, 20719, 20755, 20763, 20769, 20792, 20798, 20807, 20823, 20827, 20828, 20842, 20844, 20846 (Bab.), 20862, 20872, 20918, 20923, 20924, 20927 (commentary), 20970, 20981, 20982, 20985, 20989, 20991, 20995, 21013, 21016, 21023, 21026, 21033, 21047, 21055, 21056, 21059, 21063 (Bab.), 21065, 21087, 21089, 21091 (Bab.), 21111, 21113, 21115, 21137, 21139, 21148, 21151, 21153, 21157, 21159, 21169, 21177, 21178, 21186, 21191, 21198, 21204, 21212, 21217, 21229 (Bab.), 21251, 21262, 21263, 21272, 21273, 21279, 21280, 21296, 21312, 21313, 21324, 21336 (Bab.), 21340, 21370, 21466, 21484, 21492, 21504, 21508, 21513, 21514, 21517, 21521, 21528 (Bab), 21539, 21572, 21580, 21591, 21609, (Bab.), 21612, 21624 (Bab.), 21630, 21641 (Bab.), 21661, 21663, 21666, 21668, 21670, 21671, 21675, 21681, 21682, 21683, 21686 (Bab.), 21687 (Bab.), 21690, 21693 (Bab.), 21697, 21699, 21700, 21710, 21715, 21728, 21730, 21734, 21743, 21746, 21757, 21761, 21767, 21777, 21805, 21806, 21818, 21819, 21860 (Bab.), 21872, 21895, 21898, 21911, 21912 (Bab.), 21916, 21917, 21925, 21928, 21931, 21932, 21936, 21937 (Bab.), 21943, 21944, 21945 (Bab.), 21947, 21952, 21955, 21959, 21962, 21995, 21999 (Bab.), 22019, 22026 (Bab.), 22036, 22040, 22044, 22049, 22050, 22053, 22068, 22095 (Bab.), 22098 (Bab.), 22121 (Bab.), 22124, 22130, 22133, 22142, 22147, 22148, 22166, 22175, 22182, BM 30011, 131653, 131655

oracle questions: 17607, 17651, 18649, 19077 (Bab.), 19197 (Bab.), 20671, 20951, 20953, 21080, BM 79035